Australian born Tam Rodwell resides in London with his wife and family, two pairs of jeans and 26 white T-shirts. When he isn't writing he enjoys surfing any chance he gets.

www.tamrodwell.com

DAREDEVIL
DADS

Tam Rodwell

CRUX
PUBLISHING

Published in 2018 by Crux Publishing Ltd.

ISBN: 978-1-909979-64-2

Requests for permission to reproduce material from this work should be sent to:

hello@cruxpublishing.co.uk

CONTENTS

For Telen

ACKNOWLEDGEMENTS

I was fortunate to have a lot of help putting together *Daredevil Dads* with the generous gift of time and enthusiasm of many people. To Maggie Meade, Christopher Lascelles, David G. Llewelyn and my mum Pamela Rodwell who formed the core support group who made this happen. To Cain Lazenby, Stephanie Lawrence, Neil Thompson, Stephanie Camarena, Telen Rodwell, Kimball Taylor, Lisa Dorian, Clint Mayo, Jarrod Dunn, Martin Simpson, Jesse James Miller, Helen Lait, Kayla Layton, Audrey Critchlow, Deborah Armstrong and talented photographers J. Grant Brittain, Bryce Kanights, Ian Collins and Tom de Peyret for help finding all the missing pieces of a very big puzzle. Of course special thanks to my lovely wife Louise and our little people Lilly-Josephine and Huey – as well as their three other doting grandparents Josephine, Larry and Neal who all know I can get a little distracted and crazy at times. Lastly to Fran, Zosia, Micka, Małgorzata, Piotr and Javi and all the staff at the Hollywood Road "office" for always making me feel welcome whenever I looked up from my screen for long enough.

FOREWORD

by Krysten Knievel

Growing up with the surname Knievel, I was aware of my family history from a very early age. Although my grandfather was no longer jumping and performing by the time I was born, my family was always surrounded by the legacy he created. He was always just Grandpa to me and I have many fond memories of him.

One day he randomly called me and said he was in Chicago, and he wanted to take me to dinner. I remember hopping in a taxi and riding out to the northern suburbs, all the while thinking, "I wonder how much this cab ride is going to cost". Money was never an object for my grandfather. After dinner Grandpa then decided he would drive me home in his extremely large Winnebago RV. The streets in my neighbourhood were very narrow but he somehow managed to take every twist and turn without clipping any parked cars. I was amazed. But, if anyone could successfully drive a giant RV down the narrow streets of Chicago, it was Evel Knievel.

As a child, I knew about the stunts my grandfather had pursued and the fame he enjoyed. However, it wasn't until I was a bit older that I truly understood his legacy and the impact that he had, and continues to have, in the world of extreme sports to this day. It's funny in a way to think about my grandfather as an action figure you could purchase in the local toy shop, complete with motorcycle and his unique red, white and blue stunt leathers. He was truly an icon and a hero to a certain generation of young girls and boys who were fortunate enough to have witnessed the amazing death-defying feats he attempted as the world's most famous daredevil.

Apart from the fact that my father was a motorcycle jumper, my childhood was fairly normal. My dad had followed in my grandfather's footsteps and began his career as a daredevil when he was just eight years old. Either the daredevil gene skipped a generation, or I've seen the aftermath of one too many motorcycle stunts gone wrong, because I have zero interest in carrying out my father's and grandfather's daredevil legacy. I can remember the anxiety and nausea deep in the pit of my stomach the mornings before his big jumps. This worry used to last all the way until the moment he landed safely on the other side. I was nervous for him every single time and cried out of pure relief every time he landed. Sometimes he would crash, or sometimes land and fall off his Honda CR 500 and slide several yards on his back across the pavement tearing through his thick leather jumpsuit, giving him 'road rash'. On other occasions he would get a concussion or sometimes break a bone. But most of the time he was successful and every landing was spot on.

I specifically remember a jump my dad completed in Michigan one summer. I had driven up from Chicago to see him perform. He had fallen from his dirt bike during a wheelie run in the middle of his performance as the weather conditions had been bad. He kept saying "my shoulder is killing me" but he went ahead and jumped over all those cars in the casino parking lot. When he landed, he was still in pain and rushed himself to the hospital. There the doctors informed him that he had dislocated his shoulder before the jump. Think about that for a moment and you'll really understand the kind of man my dad is.

He is the biggest badass I've ever known but can also be the sweetest and most sensitive person. He has two completely different sides to him and I am a firm believer that his childhood and the experience of growing up as the 'son of Evel Knievel' definitely shaped him into the person he has become. As I read through the pages of this book I can't help but think about all the other children of these daredevil dads. I'm sure, just like me, there are parts of them that love having a superhero as a father, but also parts that wish they didn't have to worry about them coming home at night in one piece, or even coming home at all.

Growing up a Knievel wasn't always the glamorous life that people imagine, but I wouldn't change it for the world. My dad was and still is my biggest hero. I always knew that there was something different inside of him that made him do the things he did. Although I worried about him all the time I consider myself very lucky to be his daughter and to have seen him achieve all the things he has done with his life.

INTRODUCTION

When you're a young child dreaming of your future, nothing seems impossible. Flying to the moon, climbing the tallest mountains, riding the biggest waves – they all seem quite possible. It's only when we all get a little older that we realise that those dreams we had as children, while not impossible, were perhaps a little bit harder to obtain than we thought, and most of us settle into adulthood forgetting about them.

For some young kids, though, the lure and promise of adventure proves too great, and they spend their entire lives chasing adventure and living life on the edge, just as they dreamed of when they were younger.

What became very apparent in the hundreds of hours I spent talking to and writing about these men is that they don't actually think that what they do is dangerous. You'll discover that no matter what their jobs throw at them, no matter how many bones they break or concussions or near-death experiences they undergo, these are never going to stop them doing what they love. It certainly left me marvelling at how any of them managed to get through life alive.

The book also delves into their experiences as fathers. Parenting, as you'll discover, levels the playing field no matter who you are. You see, at 3am, when a baby is crying, no one cares that you can jump fourteen buses on a motorbike.

I
THE ASTRONAUT

It's hard for humanity as a whole not to see itself as anything other than the centre of the universe. After all, it's not as if we have any neighbours on nearby planets that come over to visit; well, none that we know of anyway. When we gaze into the night sky, we see the stars as if they surround us rather than the reality that we are barely a grain of sand scattered somewhere on the longest beach you could ever imagine.

Carl Sagan – who might reasonably be called the Albert Einstein of astronomy – was perhaps one of the first in his field to describe our minuscule existence in a way that made your average guy on the street look up and wonder what his purpose here really was. This pivotal moment came at a time when the spacecraft *Voyager 1* was just on the fringes of our galaxy, at the start of an infinite journey through the outer reaches of space. Although not an employee of NASA, Carl nevertheless carried a fair degree of clout, and successfully convinced them to turn the craft around and take one last photo of Earth. This would be the last photo it ever took on the mission; as it left our solar system, the computer controlling the camera was repurposed.

The image it captured famously became known as "the pale blue dot" – Sagan's own term – because Earth was just a flicker of light from that distance, like a particle of dust caught in a moonbeam. This photo showed all the planets of our solar system except those that weren't quite visible in that spectrum. It would be easy to devote an entire chapter to what one of the world's greatest minds had to impart to mankind before he died in 1996, but this is its essence:

In an anthropological sense, he talked about how frequently misunderstandings between cultures result in endless cycles of hatred and violence in our eagerness to kill each other and assert our dominance over our perceived universe. What the pale blue dot photo captured was the fact that Earth is merely a tiny spot in the vastness of the cosmos.

Colonel Michael Fossum is a sixty-year-old retired astronaut whose stellar career included working at NASA for twenty-seven years. During that time, he spent almost 194 days in space on three separate missions, as well as logging almost fifty hours on spacewalks outside both the space shuttle and the international space station. On his final mission in 2011, and after the previous crew had departed, he actually served as commander of the international space station.

Colonel Fossum's story is a tale of a young boy, raised in a poor area on the Mexican border in the southern USA, who dreamed about flying to the stars. He waited almost forty years to fulfil his dream – an experience that no amount of money could ever buy.

He grew up in a Texas family, which he describes as middle-class, although only at a stretch. There wasn't a lot of money, and his parents, Merlyn and Pat, had to work incredibly hard to support their family.

Mike recalls being woken up in the middle of the night many times to either gather around the radio or television for updates on the latest space mission. He still vividly remembers the moment when, as a twelve-year-old boy, he decided he wanted to go into space. He was on a school camping trip to southern Texas, near the Mexican border, away from the bright lights of civilisation. After the campfire had dwindled he found himself staring up at the stars, and that was the moment, he says, he decided what he wanted to do with his life. He is at pains to point out, however, that at that time it was an impossible dream, at least for a boy of his modest background. Even though his parents were supportive, as he grew up he found that sharing his dream with others often resulted in him being openly mocked. He eventually stopped talking about it and even stopped thinking about it. But the dream never went away; it was just compartmentalised as something he thought he would never realise.

Mike is a really upbeat kind of guy who exudes enthusiasm. But behind the fun and laughter is one heck of a driven individual who worked his socks off to get to where he is today. During college he put his dream of walking in space somewhat out of his mind and after graduating he joined the US Air Force as an engineer. By a twist of fate, he found himself posted to the Johnson Space Centre in Houston, where he was effectively employed by NASA to provide support for Mission Control.

At this time, in 1982, the space shuttle programme was still in its infancy, and he found himself involved in the beginnings of an exciting new chapter of human space exploration. Over the coming months, the new recruit was quick to make friends. Luckily for Mike, he discovered that the astronauts' office was just down the hall from his own, and over the coming months his enthusiasm and attitude caught the attention of two of the programme's most experienced astronauts, Jerry Ross and Ellison Onizuka. The pair, he says, took him under their wing and encouraged him to pursue his dream of space travel. Guided by Ross and Onizuka, he enrolled in test pilot school as part of the air force – a path taken by many astronauts in order to get their wings. In his own words he says he left NASA "on fire", his childhood dream completely reignited. After having put his dreams of space flight on hold for so long, he felt as if he was finally on his way.Sadly, though, less than a year later, Ellison Onizuka was killed in the space shuttle Columbia disaster. A good friend was lost, but he is grateful beyond words for the great man's mentoring and friendship.

Even though Mike followed the best path he could, it still took him thirteen years and five separate interviews from entering test pilot school to finally booking his ticket to space. Through the many failed applications Mike just put his head down and kept plugging away. His family lived through it with him as well, although the disappointments were never dwelt upon and were rarely spoken about. His children knew what he was trying to achieve and that was all that mattered, whether he made it or not. It was also a chance to show them, just as his father had shown him, that if you work very hard, good things can come to you and dreams can be realised.

Of his time in space he says he was very overwhelmed with the experience of his first spacewalk. There were no support structures or scuba divers as in the training facility back on Earth, and just a narrow handrail to hold onto in the great abyss of space. While he has never had any issues with heights it was unnerving to be 240 miles off the Earth's surface and feeling quite vulnerable. While he was able to view space through the space shuttle's windows, nothing quite prepares you, he says, to seeing it with your head inside a big goldfish bowl helmet, vastness in every direction.

The most unnerving moment of seven spacewalks was the time he was riding on the end of a fifty-foot boom arm attached to the end of the fifty-foot space shuttle robotic arm. This was part of a test to see if the whole extension could hold an astronaut stable enough to conduct repairs on the space shuttle orbiter's heat shield. He was effectively a guinea pig for this experiment, and a very long way away from the safety of his space residence.

It's different from the training you do underwater, and it takes as much energy to stop your motion as it does to begin it in the first place.

Obviously one of the biggest dangers associated with space walks is the loss of oxygen supply. It can happen in a number of ways but it will almost always happen very slowly, and astronauts must be able to spot the signs. Such are the concentration levels, it isn't always as easy as it sounds. All astronauts undergo rigorous training in this regard. You can't call time out in space and if you suddenly find yourself low on air it takes some time to get back to the safety of the shuttle or space station.

Mike has been a retired astronaut for almost a year now, and while he looks back on his career with pride, it's also with bitter sweetness as he knows he'll never slide out of an airlock into the vastness of space again. Those images, though, are burned into his memory and impossible to erase or forget, and he admits catching himself daydreaming about that time in his life.

Mike loves to talk about his time in space, and he has an endless supply of quirky tales about what it's like to live in zero gravity. Firstly, Mike mentions, with his characteristic laugh, that space is a great place to live if you are a little vain. Zero gravity means that your face can no longer head south. It appears much rounder and suppler, and most of those wrinkles and eye bags get nicely ironed out, taking years off. He says that the first time he visited space, he couldn't believe his luck when he looked in the mirror and saw a fresh-faced version of himself staring back. The effects don't survive the return missions unfortunately, as your face reverts to normal as soon as you re-enter Earth's atmosphere.

Although he is a good-looking man even without the "space facelift", he tends not to dwell too much on the miraculous fountain of youth. One can grow up to five centimetres in height, as the spine relaxes and the whole body stretches out. I joke with him that it all sounds very *in vogue* in that everyone is wrinkle-free and six feet tall. It's not all glamour of course, as there are no showers in space, something he really missed. Water can't find the drain, he says; it just floats around in the air like blobs of jelly. Apparently, you can wash your hair without getting your collar wet, which sounds fairly interesting.

The other thing he regularly missed while in space was fresh food – especially vegetables – as everything is vacuum-packed, of course, resembling those baby food pouches you see in supermarkets. He openly admits he also missed pizza and beer, a comment that certainly gives him the human touch.

There is no getting away from the dangers of space. Mike knows the stakes were high and the risk was immense. He lost some friends on the way and was always aware that he and the crew could become a fireball in seconds, thereby handing him a fate over which he had absolutely no control.

Of course, you can't talk to an astronaut and not ask about the two space shuttle disasters – Challenger and Columbia. Challenger was, of course, the better-known disaster, simply because millions of people were watching it on television when it exploded seventy-three seconds after take-off in 1986. In 2003, Columbia was destroyed on re-entering the Earth's atmosphere, too far away to be visible. No one embarking on a career at NASA can have any illusions about how serious the consequences are should something go wrong – although, with the huge advancements in technology and safety, it is a far better prospect today than it was a few decades ago.

Despite the dangers, the lure of space travel is just too great for some, and regardless of the risk, just like Mike, they will do whatever is necessary to book their place for take-off. Mike says that Columbia, particularly, had a profound effect on both him and his family. Through his work at NASA, his family knew some of the children whose parents perished in the accident. Although Mike hadn't yet been to space at that time, he was on course to do so, and his children were old enough to recognise the possibility of their father dying in the same way. They had all grown up with him constantly applying to become an astronaut, so it was just accepted that it was what he was going to do.

One of the greatest risks of space travel comes from hazards that can't be seen. Mike talks about the vast quantity of rubbish which has been discarded in space during the many years of exploration. There are now millions of pieces of debris whizzing around the planet at speeds of up to 17,500 mph. It's estimated that at least 500,000 of those pieces are at least the size of a marble. This might not sound like much, he says, but at the speed they are travelling, it would most certainly spell disaster if they were to hit and penetrate the wrong part of the space shuttle. Marble-size bullets are relatively large compared to the smaller but equally deadly ones that are neither visible nor trackable by NASA. The reinforced windows of the space shuttle have had to be replaced regularly over the years given that a simple fleck of paint has enough potential force to damage them. Even a sphere of aluminium around one millimetre in diameter can inflict as much damage as a .22 calibre bullet. Anything larger than ten centimetres would be the equivalent of a flying stick of dynamite with the potential to destroy an entire space station.

Whether it's debris in space or plastics in the ocean, humans unfortunately leave their mark wherever they go.

For every astronaut, retirement always brings a certain amount of depression, as they know that their time in space is over. Even winning the battle over those mental lows, they're still faced with the obvious physical ones as they try to come to terms with getting used to living within the constraints of gravity. Zero gravity makes you feel like superman, he says, and when you get back to Earth everything is so much harder to do. Upon his return, lifting his legs to walk or lifting a cup to his mouth suddenly became very strenuous activities.

His readjustment to life on Earth was helped enormously by the strong support of his family. The hard work his wife put into keeping the family together during his long missions is not lost on him. He says they have now, in a way, started a new chapter in their lives. There are no more space missions and as the kids have since flown the nest, they are both enjoying a slightly slower pace of life these days.

Surprisingly, during his time at NASA, Mike was always fairly reluctant to tell people he was an astronaut. The personal rewards, he says, were more than enough for him and he never wanted it to seem like he was bragging. Generally, whenever anyone asked what he did, he would say he was an engineer at NASA, which wasn't a lie, but nor was it the whole truth.

His wife, Melanie, however, was typically the opposite. She'd regularly nudge him in the ribs, saying, 'Go on. Tell them you're an astronaut.' He did not mind that as he's happy that she is proud of him enough to want to say that. His kids are a bit more reserved, like him, and only referred to his job as the *A-word*. They enjoyed what he did but in a private way, and they did not broadcast it to their school friends. That secrecy, if you want to call it that, could backfire at times. For years he volunteered with the scouts' organisation, and in the company of all the other parents involved he would simply say he was an engineer at NASA. The truth sort of came out naturally, as it's a little hard for people not to find out when you leave Earth to spend five months in space. He knows the fact that he never really disclosed his job put a few noses out of joint, but he's always liked to fly under the radar.

One of his favourite family photos is one with his wife and children huddled together around his youngest child, Kenneth, who was eight at the time, with the rocket blasting off in the background. The young fellow was having difficulty dealing with his father's departure, and Mike says the photo reminds him just how much he sacrificed in order to do what he did. Although it pains him to do so, he admits that pursuing the dream of flying to the stars requires a degree of selfishness. Mike says that whilst he was being blasted into space on the top of what was essentially a very large bomb, the most courageous people are the ones on the ground watching their loved ones disappear into the stratosphere.

In the world of space travel, there are a lot fewer near-miss stories than would be expected for more terrestrial activities. When things go wrong in space, they go wrong in a very big way, and people simply don't come home.

Mike teaches astronomy to Boy Scouts, so is very familiar with the constellations which are easily visible from the ground. He was shocked to find it difficult to find the constellations he knew so well because there are so many stars visible in space. The stars also don't twinkle in space like they do when viewed from Earth because our atmosphere has lots of tiny suspended particles of dust that the starlight has to pass through, which gives the impression they are twinkling.

I'd often wondered why stars are not always visible when looking at photos of space but Mike let me know that this only applies when passing through sunlight. Without an atmosphere above you, the sun's light is incredibly intense, and it forces the iris to compensate by narrowing down and limiting the amount of light entering your eyes (or camera). As a result, you'll see the space station or Earth below with great clarity, but be unable to discern the stars, and the sky above looks totally black, with the exception of the moon. Out of sunlight though, he says it's an incredible visual spectacle – especially the Milky Way.

As I researched Mike's life, what becomes apparent quite early on is that he's taken everything life has to offer. But he's been just as busy giving back as well. He learned from the best, as his own dad was a hard-working, salt-of-the-earth kind of guy who played a role in the leadership of their church when they were growing up. His dad also ran many projects that benefited disadvantaged members of the community. However, sadly, he passed away in an aeroplane crash at the age of 51 and never got to see his son blast off into space.

Mike has four children: Carrie (33), Mitch (31), John (27), and Kenneth (21). He's tried his best to raise them in the same way he was, which involved teaching them about the importance of a good work ethic as well as taking responsibility for your own actions. He's been heavily involved in the Boy Scouts of America for most of his life, and has seen all his boys pass through its halls. He says of the young boys involved in his troupe that about twenty percent of them don't have fathers and therefore really benefit from having a reliable male role model to look up to.

Mike talks with the kind of common sense you wish you would hear from politicians, but never actually do, and I'd guess he's never entertained any kind of *band aid* solutions. Mike also has the distinguished honour of having a school named after him in Texas. There are a few videos of visits he's made to the school over the years, and it's obvious, even many years later, that he is still extraordinarily humble about his achievements. In this day and age, people may dream of having a star on the Hollywood walk of fame, or a vast monetary reward for a job well done, but what could be more fulfilling than to have your name adorn the front of a centre for education?

That's not to say that he's totally infallible. He cites a tale of parenthood where it all went very badly wrong and it was down to his own mistake. He and his youngest daughter, Carrie, who was three at the time, came across what looked like an electric fence during a walk in a wooded area. Strangely, he says, his natural curiosity made him reach out and grab the fence, which gave him a fairly mild jolt – not particularly unpleasant if you were expecting it. He then decided to explain to Carrie what an electric fence was, and beckoned her to touch the wire. She was amused by the strange sensation it gave her. They then hatched a cunning plan to give Mum – Melanie – a little surprise, and called her to join them. When she arrived, she was asked to hold Carrie's hand; Carrie then grabbed the wire. Mike, also holding his wife's hand, then grabbed what he thought was the same wire. Unfortunately, it was the wrong one, and set to a much higher voltage. Such was the shock that it blasted the trio off their feet and only now, many years later, can he laugh about the incident.

Disregarding electric fences Mike says he has had several profound experiences staring out of the space shuttle, but one of the most interesting was the way he had his view of the world challenged. He describes the realisation that seeing the Earth in books or as desktops globes, with defined borders and countries differentiated by colour, you get a completely false impression of how it really looks. He was struck by the "oneness" of Earth…

'We are all spinning around on a ball of compacted space dust, and not separated by borders, cultures or beliefs as we often perceive ourselves to be.'

He said he never grew tired of staring through the window, and he was able to clearly distinguish cities like London or Paris, just by how well they were lit up at night. It wasn't all beautiful, though, as you see some pretty disturbing things from space. On the island of Madagascar, which has suffered massive deforestation, you can witness the effects of erosion, where very little remains to hold the soil together. Huge plumes of mud are visible from space, cascading into the surrounding ocean almost as if the island is being eaten alive. Similarly, in the Amazon rain forest you can see the immediate effect when a new road is cut. It becomes like a cancerous growth, as the road gives access to loggers and they move in and fell the trees on either side. He says it really opened his eyes to what we are doing to our home, and how we all need to think about the toll our greed is taking on the planet.

His longest stint on the international space station of 167 days was well timed. A period of high solar activity for our Sun made for amazing views of the *Aurora Australis* or Southern lights. At times the dancing waves of red and green lights made it up to their orbiting height, so they passed through it as it went around them. He was at pains to try and figure out a way to properly capture it, and eventually succeeded. The videos he made are now viewable all over the Internet, and he's very proud to have been able to share that amazing show with the rest of the planet.

Perhaps it was talk of profound experiences or the book's subject matter but Mike had clearly been thinking about things before we spoke. He began, unprompted, by saying that even though he has had a blessed and successful life, he has some regrets regarding the way he raised his children. He says that during their formative years, he never allowed himself time away from his work and the pursuit of his dreams to take the children on the kind of holidays he'd been fortunate enough to share with his own parents. He talks very openly about being bundled with his siblings into a car, towing a rickety old caravan all over the USA, and how fondly he looks back on those times. They were low-budget vacations certainly, but the kind of close family time where the clocks and bedtime routines get thrown out the window, and everyone just enjoys the moment. While he still enjoyed many vacations with his brood, it was never for more than a week, as he simply couldn't remove himself from his job and his dream for longer than that. It's definitely something that had played on his mind over the years, but then again, these things always do for those blessed with a high degree of self-awareness. Perhaps he didn't get the balance between work and family perfect, but who ever does?

Regardless of these regrets, it certainly doesn't seem to have had any negative effect on the family he has created with his wife. Their children are happy, healthy and have excelled in everything they have done thus far. However, Mike and Melanie do have the odd sleepless night as their eldest son, Mitch, a fighter pilot with the US Air Force, is stationed in the Middle East. Flying regularly in that volatile part of the world is about as unpredictable as you can get. He says his son's occupation and current posting has certainly given him food for thought in terms of what he put his family through when he was on space missions.

I ask him if this is maybe some kind of karma coming back to haunt him…to which he laughs and says,

'I don't really think I'd call it karma. We are just happy he's doing what he loves doing, and so long as he comes home safe that's the only concern we have.'

Throughout our interviews Mike has been refreshingly candid about his life and experiences. It was a little difficult to find a suitable way to close the chapter, other than with this:

It may surprise you but astronauts in the Western world are required to learn Russian as an important part of their training, and it is a very hard language to master. While he doesn't profess to be a linguistic genius, he does enjoy being able to have a conversation as well as discuss technical matters. In the West we get so used to the fact that most far-flung places we visit roll out the "English menu", so to speak, and make it very easy for us to get by. Space is completely different, and that space station circling the Earth is a collaboration between some of the biggest and most powerful countries on Earth that don't always see eye to eye in a lot of other ways.

He says that being a part of that re-affirmed to him that humanity as a whole can achieve some amazing things if we all work together. It saddens him a little, he says, that back on *terra firma* everyone nowadays seems so angry and falling out over what, in the grand scheme of things, are very minor differences. We all seem, he says, too willing to burn bridges with our neighbours instead of trying to mend fences for a better life for ourselves and our children. Too many people complain without doing anything about it. Mike, though, has so far put his money where his mouth is.

Having raised four very well-rounded humans himself, he nevertheless still takes the time to help young boys who weren't lucky enough to have the same sort of stable family background. He's also inspired the next generation of space travellers through his missions, as well as through his frequent visits to schools. It's little wonder then that he ended up in education, and now sits as Chief Operating Officer of Texas A&M University at Galveston, having retired from NASA.

Having come from a relatively underprivileged home, he's certainly done very well for himself, and he's busier than he ever was. He still admits to the odd daydream in his office, but it's a different dream from that of the young boy who gazed up into the stars. Mike is living proof that no matter what your background, if you put your mind to something and work hard, you can make those dreams come true.

"Life in a tin can"

II
THE SMOKE JUMPER

L ittle is known or understood about the obscure profession of smoke jumping despite it being perhaps the most elite of all firefighting positions. So rare a breed are smoke jumpers that in the whole of the United States there are less than four hundred and fifty of them working in the field at any given time.

A smoke jumper's role is to parachute into areas of wilderness affected by forest fires and attempt, by hand, to extinguish smaller newly ignited fires before they take hold and grow. The fires they are tasked to deal with lie in areas that are not accessible by road or by any other means other than aeroplane. Spotting these small, barely visible fires is a big part of the art of smoke jumping as they often emit only a very small cloud of smoke in their infancy. As a result, the team in the air face a very big challenge to find them.

There is no getting away from just how deadly the pursuit is. Smoke jumpers parachute from incredibly low altitudes of as little as 1000ft which gives them zero room for error should their chute not deploy correctly. The areas they land in are also usually densely wooded, which means they need to land with pinpoint accuracy otherwise death is a real possibility. There are no fire hoses for this hardy bunch though; once landed, their tools such as axes and shovels are dropped nearby and used to dig a mineral line in the earth or for clearing wooded areas of combustible materials. This essentially creates a barrier over which the flames cannot cross for lack of fuel to burn. If that fails, they sometimes need to back burn areas to achieve the same outcome – in essence, fighting fire with fire. The work is extraordinarily difficult and they are also under immense mental strain having to constantly be aware of the changing weather and approaching fires that can come from any direction.

As far as smoke jumpers or firefighters go, you won't find any more experienced than Johnny Yount. As a native of North California he has been fighting fires for almost fifty years. Fires in California can often appear to have split personalities. A mixture of trade winds and the dry climate can instantly turn a humble bonfire into a raging fireball in a very short period of time. In this part of the world it's not a case of "if" you'll see a huge wildfire, but more about "when". Although these days Johnny is no longer jumping out of planes he's still involved in the day-to-day work of fire management. Fire is in his blood and even at the age of seventy-one he shows no sign of slowing down.

Much of his career has also been spent fighting fires from the air – using huge planes to dump large amounts of water on blazes. Like smoke jumping, it's equally perilous and he's had many close shaves with death. A skilled pilot, he has flown just about everything that has wings.

It's actually quite difficult to define Johnny's main occupation in firefighting, as he has basically done just about everything. He's been a smokejumper, driven your standard land-based fire engines as well as piloting planes in aerial firefighting. He has also been part of *Helitack* crews, which is similar to smoke jumping but involves helicopters for landing firefighting teams. Essentially if there was a forest fire in Northern California in the last fifty years then this man either knew about it or was involved in putting it out. His actions have indirectly saved many thousands of lives and an incalculable number of properties and livestock.

The man himself is a tad shy of the limelight as all true heroes are. I learn, remarkably, that he's never really discussed the details of what he does with his wife, Laverne, and daughter, Tracy. Of course, they know what he does and did do for a job but the perilous details were never really discussed over the dinner table. You could say, in a sense, that he almost led a Batman/Bruce Wayne type existence – a mild-mannered, attentive father and husband at home. Then he morphed into a firefighting demon upon arrival at work, flying and jumping out of planes and saving lives along the way. To get a sense of this man you really need to understand how he started out. It's really a story about a very young boy who was obsessed with fire and spent his whole life hunting it down.

As a young child Johnny's parents part-owned a crop dusting company in the central valley of California. His father had retired after twenty-five years of military service that included two wars and become a volunteer fireman. He occasionally took the young boy with him on emergencies. In retrospect, Johnny thinks he was probably only about ten years old at the time.

He loved aeroplanes, and the firefighting was always exciting to watch from a distance, although he admits he was always trying to inch closer. There were negatives, however, which included his father being the first on the scene of horrific car accidents. Although he tried to shield Johnny from the scenes, Johnny says he started to develop a numbness to the horrific injuries he saw and watching people die traumatic deaths right before his eyes.

By the time he was in his late teens, Johnny had several first aid certificates and had been present at hundreds of fire and accident emergencies. His mum wasn't so cool at the idea of him accompanying his father to road accidents and fires, but accepted his choices because of the dedication he showed. At the same time, the young boy was developing a real obsession for aeroplanes. By fourteen he had already (illegally) soloed his first aircraft. At sixteen he received his student's pilot licence and by seventeen had a private pilot's licence. Johnny is quick to point out that he actually graduated high school with very poor results, which meant that once he received his commercial pilot's licence on his eighteenth birthday, his path was decided. That's not to say that he didn't have his share of misadventure during his formative years learning to fly. He recalls with much laughter the time he went a bit off-course during a training flight and attempted what fans of the *Top Gun* movie might call a fly-by. Given a strict boundary within which to fly by his instructor he decided to stretch the rules a little and attempt to fly over the family house some six miles out of his training zone. As the excited youngster approached the house he spied his mother hanging out the washing and in his attempts to fly over as low as possible he clipped the wing of his plane on the only tree within a square mile. After the initial shock of the near crash had passed he looked down to see his mother laid out on the ground. Fearing that some debris had hit and killed her he limped back to the airfield in a state of shock. On arrival, he was told that his mother was in fact alive and well and had called to ask if he got back okay.

Apparently, the shock of the loud noise created by the plane hitting the tree had caused her blood vessels to constrict and she had passed out from the shock. It's a tale that was told over and over again when he was growing up, and it never ceases to bring a smile to his face even some fifty-odd years later. He's adamant, despite a few hiccups here and there, that he chose the best career for himself and it was all he ever wanted to do.

'Flying and firefighting were never forced on me. From crop dusting to aerial firefighting I've loved every minute of it and it never really felt like a job to me.'

Johnny describes his time as a smoke jumper as just like any other job despite its obvious perils. An apprenticeship in dangerous activities is almost actually required to get your foot in the door, but knowledge of firefighting in general is a big part of who is, and isn't, accepted into the programme. There can't be, as Johnny says any holes in your knowledge of fire. Otherwise, you'll simply be found out and pose a risk not only to yourself but to other members of the team. These teams aren't just parachuting in for a few hours' work either, as they know once they leave the safety of the plane they could be on the ground for up to forty-eight hours. They carry on their backs large kits (weighing anything up to 150 lbs) that include a sleeping bag, water and meal provisions to last the duration. Unbelievably, they are also prone to being hit by lightning as well; it does not help that they are often the only people working in thousands of hectares of wilderness, wielding metal tools. If lightning needed a target, then this is as good as it's going to get.

Tales of death-defying jumps from planes at low altitudes flow thick and fast, as you would expect from a man with his experience. He recalls one of his more memorable call-outs in the Sacramento Valley in California during the high season when danger zones were spilling into the red, day after day. This particular day had all the right ingredients for spot fires taking hold: extraordinarily hot, coupled with a weather pattern extending from the Gulf of Mexico, bringing billowing cumulus clouds up through the densely forested valleys. It was, Johnny says, the perfect conditions for lightning to strike and the team was on red alert waiting to see when and where that would be. When the call did come it was in an area about thirty miles from the base and reports were of a blaze of less than an acre. Luckily, the thunderstorm had slowed the pace of the fire, but they knew it wouldn't be long before it dried and the fire started spreading. Turbulence is not uncommon in these types of weather patterns and sitting on the floor of the aircraft, Johnny recalls being thrown up and down and sideways, knowing it wouldn't be long till air sickness kicked in. He also recalls the impending fear of the trip and peering out of the windows into the dense and mountainous terrain and hoping this wasn't the spot he would be required to jump.

Next thing he knows, the *spotter*, who is in charge of operations, is throwing streamers out of the window to check for wind drift and it's time to jump. It's a small cabin, and a narrow time frame to exit. He's got to get close enough to the other jumpers to fall in unison without bumping them out the door before they are ready to go. A little like an analogy of dominoes that fall perfectly but never quite touch. On this particular jump, they are only 1,000 ft from the ground, which is quite common, so there is very little time to think or react as the hang time in the air until landing can be as little as two minutes. Johnny well knows the only thing that's on any jumper's mind is the landing spot. In this case, it's a mere 40 x 40 feet of opening in the timber below, but unfortunately, on this occasion, he realises mid-descent that the winds have not been kind and he's not going to make it. Trying to land in a patch of 150-ft trees isn't ideal and he knows it, but he's been here before and is well versed. With legs clamped tightly together he "javelins" himself into the tree tops and hopes for the best as he waits for that inevitable moment when the branches catch the parachute and leave him suspended. On this particular occasion, he finds himself some thirty feet from the ground with no other way to get down other than cutting the parachute free from himself and plummeting to the ground. It's a very intense part of smoke jumping and one needs to be very calm during the process to free oneself safely.

There is, Johnny says, a special knife that smoke jumpers carry especially for this purpose. What's most important is that they check to see if any of the ropes have become entangled around their neck. Once they cut the rope they know they are going to go down fast, and a mislaid rope could effectively mean instant death. Luckily, on this occasion, he survives and makes a comfortable landing.

16th Birthday Record— 14 Solos In 14 Planes

SOLO MARATHON — John Yount is sent aloft on his first solo by Bob Swann, his instructor. Below is his 16th birthday was over. He had soloed in 14 different types of planes, setting a new world's record. (Signal photo)

The unique thing about smoke jumping is that once on the ground after a traumatic landing, that's when the real work starts and they attempt to either put out spot fires or try and contain larger blazes. The key, Johnny says, is clearing areas around the fires that take away potential fuel sources like dried foliage or excess timber. In almost all cases, it's actually not possible to put out the fires even if they are only small as they simply don't have the volume of water. Effectively, they look at these small fires as beasts that need to be caged and they do that by taking away their life force and letting them slowly burn themselves out.

All experienced smoke jumpers know that they exist on a knife edge and while attempting to contain the fires, also need to try and stay alive. When they take off, fires can move faster than a person can run so smoke jumpers always have an eye peeled, waiting and watching for new blazes to appear on the horizon. Planes periodically drop fresh supplies of water, food and equipment to them when needed, as well as maps that tell them where they are and the best way to return to civilisation. Johnny says on several occasions he and the team had to walk for a whole day to get to a place from where they could be collected. Often that distance, as the crow flies, wasn't that long but given the terrain they had to forge their way through it could be extremely slow-going. It was tough work, and tougher still knowing that you could no sooner get back to the comforts of modern living than you'd get another call to do it all again.

He talks openly and fondly about his time working in these teams and the deep bond he shared with the other men. You are, he says, relying on each other to stay alive and that is trust on a very epic level. Of the many jumps he did, there were times he felt like he was being hunted by the fire and, on rare occasions, he felt he wasn't going to make it. Some said he was crazy for putting his life on the line for the job but to him there wasn't another option. He looked on the job as essential not only to the survival of the wilderness but also to the life of the people and the animals that lived in it. Selfless is probably the best description of what you'd call these people who do what they do. It's hard and thankless work but they thrive of the rewards of a job well done.

Johnny talks openly about the differences between fighting fires in the vast expanse of the North California wilderness as opposed to urban firefighting where you might be tackling a single burning building. Wildfires can burn for weeks, even months at a time; their fuel supply is essentially endless and in a perfect storm, he says, fires almost personify themselves as the beast intent on death and destruction. Fatigue, he explains, can become a real problem during these long blazes, and he recalls it being difficult to switch off and get rest when you knew that your fellow firefighters are still out on shift risking their lives.

This is also the point where it can go very wrong – when people have been in intense situations for long periods of time. Sometimes, he explains, miscommunications can happen when you have different teams working miles apart. He describes a fire his team was tackling in Oregon where another unit backlit a fire (this is one way firefighters tackle a controlled burn of an area to remove the fuel and stop the fire advancing), a short distance away from them. They then realised that because of that backlit fire they were now stuck in between the original fire and the one the other crew had lit. The only escape route for them was a passage down a very steep ridge all the way to the Pacific Ocean. They did make it out unscathed but it could easily have gone very wrong and he's seen that happen to others many, many times over.

'I've been on calls where we had to respond to crews that were caught in similar situations to the one in Oregon. I've seen men burned to death and others suffering from multiple broken bones as they desperately tried to flee the fire and jump over, or down whatever they had to, in a desperate attempt to escape. When a fire is moving at speed there is little you can do to outrun it and that's a situation you always want to avoid at all cost. Although I've lost friends, I've always been able to carry on. In order not to end up in an insane asylum, you kind of develop a numbness to reality. I can feel sorrow but, like fear, I don't let it control my life.'

Johnny's certainly had his share of close calls over the years but you don't need to be fighting flames to find death knocking at your door, especially when you fly an aeroplane. He tells a story about a time back in the early eighties when he was working as a crop duster in Northern California to supplement his income. On his tenth or so take-off of the day, the huge 800 hp engine in his plane suffered catastrophic failure, causing the supercharger to disintegrate and cut through the engine mounts. This in turn caused the engine to be ejected from the plane, leaving Johnny a hundred feet in the air with no power in the shell of the aircraft he was sitting in. The trip back to the ground was swift and ferocious for him; the plane was fully fuelled and carrying 4000 lbs of fertiliser, and it began dropping like a lead balloon. The plane eventually crash-landed in a field of mud executing several cartwheels in the process and ejecting Johnny, still attached to his seat, some fifty yards away. He says he lay there for some time, very concussed, and trying to decide if he had all his limbs still connected to his body but very, very thankful to still be alive.

If the crash wasn't extraordinary enough it soon became apparent that Johnny had, through the severe head injury he suffered, ignited a part of his brain he had never utilised before. He describes a day soon after his release from hospital when he went to the local store to buy food. This was before the time of price scanners, so the clerk would call out the price and punch in the amount on the register. While waiting his turn in the queue his brain was, of its own accord, internally adding up the numbers the clerk was calling out and getting the final amounts correct every time. For about three years after, and with continual medical evaluation, doctors were astounded at his new-found abilities to add huge numbers together just like a calculator. It was all the more remarkable as he had been such a poor student at school and had never ever showed any inclination towards mathematics. As his health improved and his brain healed, the condition started to leave him and the super powers of calculating he'd accidentally inherited all but disappeared. Today, no one is any the wiser as to an explanation behind the condition. Sadly, the trauma of the whole thing brought about the end of his first marriage, but fortunes reversed soon after when he met his second wife, Laverne, and they went on to have daughter, Tracey, together. It was, he says, a very happy time in their lives, all brought about by him cheating death by the most minute of fractions.

Johnny becomes very animated when he talks about his flying days. He was certainly born into a family that very much encouraged his interest and for that he believes he was very lucky. He also became a minor celebrity for his flying in the local area for a flying stunt that he carried out before he had even reached the age of thirty.

'On my birthday in 1963 I solo flew fourteen different types of aeroplanes in one day. It was a publicity stunt to draw attention to my parents' new airline business. It was actually a world record at the time and I still have the newspaper clippings to prove it. Thinking back now it all sounds too crazy to be true. I think I really was indeed born to fly.'

Publicity stunts aside, Johnny truly came into his own when piloting planes involved in aerial firefighting. As he became a little older the smoke jumping part of his life became less and less frequent and he used his encyclopaedic knowledge of all aspects of fighting blazes to extinguish them by air.

While smoke jumping had its obvious dangers, aerial firefighting seems that little bit safer to the outsider, however, nothing could be further from the truth. First and foremost, he was dealing with planes that were extraordinarily heavy given the combination load of fuel and water that he was carrying. Planes react in different ways and are harder to correct when they are bloated with load so he explains that often you needed to have faster reaction times as well as planning your turns further ahead as a result of the slight slow motion effect one needed to deal with.

Flying at low levels a few feet above the ground or the tree tops at 120 mph can be extremely dangerous, for obvious reasons. You need to be as close to the flames as possible to give the water drop the best possible chance of working. He explains the flying as constantly pulling up to miss trees or going under power lines that he could barely see, plus turning the aircraft at near stall speed hour after hour through both up and down drafts of air. It takes an immense amount of concentration and physical strength to do this work all day and there really is no let-up. Also, there is the added wildcard of smoke from the fire and from flying down narrow canyons. Violent winds can also be a problem as well, as they can shift a plane's trajectory. This is fine, he says, if you've got room to move high in the sky, but less welcome if you're near objects you could crash into.

Johnny is a very modest man and never speaks of his adventures in a way that makes them sound heroic. It's amazing to think that the stories he's discussed here will be the first time his daughter really finds out about the incredible things her father has done with his life. He's an extremely proud father and is adamant that he wouldn't change a thing about the way he has raised his daughter. He is clearly very proud of her and describes that raising her was very easy as she was always so level-headed. The balancing act between the two ladies in his life wasn't always easy but he tried to make sure he spent quality time with his wife and did activities with his daughter that she wanted to do.

Johnny describes how his own father was very fair and attentive, and loved both him and his sister unconditionally. His father then went on to have a wonderful relationship with his grandchild, which he is very proud of. He describes the satisfaction of what he does that keeps him so happy. He just likes to help people and do the right thing. 'Do as you would be done by, and all that'. He likes the fact that he helps make a difference in people's lives by saving lives and property from fire, but also that his work in the agricultural industry makes a difference. Many of the crops he's attended to in California find themselves on tables all around the world feeding families, and he likes that.

So now, at seventy-one, and a grandfather himself, what does he think the future holds? Well, he mentions that while he has a pre-paid funeral package set in place he doesn't plan on using it anytime soon. His grandson describes him as a big kid, a term he loves, and he has every intention of being around for some time yet to watch the young man grow. He still loves being involved in fire management on a day-to-day basis and will keep doing that for as long as he can. He reminisces fondly about his time as a smoke jumper and aerial firefighter. While others probably thought he needed his head examined for constantly putting himself in harm's way, he just saw it as *another day at the office* and always has done.

He admits that he does have one quirky attribute that doesn't quite fit his daredevil personality and that's when he gets behind the wheel of a car. He says he must be the only person in the whole of California who sticks rigidly to all speed limits. It drives his wife, Laverne, completely crazy, he laughs, but that's just the way he is. So, it seems that our firefighting hero isn't always the daredevil he appears to be and morphs into your quintessential Sunday driver when behind the wheel of an automobile. Maybe he got enough thrills and spills through his day job over the years to need an adrenaline top-up. What's for sure is that the state of California has been well looked after over the last half a century and it will miss his assistance when he finally hangs up his boots, whenever that may be. One suspects that whenever this takes place, it will probably be done with a fair amount of kicking and screaming.

"Fire Hunters"

III
THE BIG WAVE SURFER

©Brian Bielmann

I n the fast-paced society that we live in, everyone is doing what they can to make sure their children acquire the necessary tools to survive in life. Or have we, in this modern age, overlooked the true meaning of survival, which is being able to fend for oneself without the aid of a cash machine or a credit card? What happens one day in a few decades if the shelves run bare at the market and we have to rely on ourselves to feed hungry mouths? If you want to believe the doomsayers then yes, we will almost certainly be living in some kind of bleak, dystopian world where money won't matter as you can't eat or drink it, and we will all be fighting to the death over the last can of baked beans.

The subject of this chapter, Shane Dorian, is acknowledged not only as perhaps one of the most daring and fearless big wave surfers of all time, but he also raises his children to become involved in his *survivalist pursuits*, such as hunting for wild animals using only bows and arrows. He wants to raise his children to know where their food comes from and respect what sits on their plate come dinner time. Needless to say his celebrity status has shone a blazing light on his parenting choices.

The life of a professional big wave surfer is a ludicrously exhilarating and dangerous one, as you'd expect. These elite individuals spend their days chasing giant storms and have to be ready at a moment's notice to jump on a plane to fly halfway across the world. The perfect storms that create these giant waves of up to ninety feet are so rare and so fleeting, that to get there in the exact window of opportunity to ride them takes some serious planning and preparation. The other thing to consider is that with storm chasing nothing is guaranteed. Mother Nature is an unpredictable beast even at the best of times. Wave surfers can easily travel more than halfway around the world only to find that the swell, supposedly generated by the predicted storm, never quite made it to the scale that was necessary.

There is also the consideration when surfers arrive that the entire trip may result in only a single wave being ridden. The line-ups in some of the more famous big wave spots on earth can get a little crowded at times, such is the competition for space. But it's not just the competition that can hinder the surfer's wave count. Big wave spots are sometimes hard, no, actually they're almost always hard, to negotiate; to have a couple of fifty-foot waves land on your head and nearly drown you before you've even arrived at your starting point is immensely draining, even for the fittest in the sport.

So far has big wave surfing evolved in the last decade that there is now a special contest circuit that sees surfers compete against each other in all four corners of the globe. While a younger crowd dominates traditional, professional surfing, big wave surfing is open to older competitors. Many of the top competitors are aged in their late thirties to mid-forties with some even nudging fifty. While it seems like these days even moderately rated surfers are all flying through the air on surfboards the size of skateboards, there are still only a select few who can dust off an eleven-foot board and paddle out when the waves hit fifty feet. And while it's difficult to define who the best big wave surfer in the world is, you won't find any serious surfer's top three list that is free of Shane's name. Perhaps that's the biggest accolade any big wave surfer could have.

Shane had a very successful career on the world championship tour of surfing before he retired in 2004. He then became known almost solely for his big wave surfing prowess. For over a decade Shane shared the stage in the World Surf League with the best in the business and won numerous events. So fierce is the competition that many potential world-beating, talented surfers spend their entire career on the circuit and never trouble the podium as it's so tough. I asked Shane if he had ever wondered what would happen after he retired from the "young man's game" of the WSL tour, given that back then the big wave tour didn't quite exist yet...

I think the highlight is that my surfing career is still happening. I expected it to be over when I was thirty, so all these extra years have been a pleasant surprise. To think that I still get paid for what I love to do at my age is amazing.'

It's typically humble candour from a man who's lifted more of those oversize cheques than anyone else at various big wave awards ceremonies over the years. These events honour the biggest or heaviest waves ridden in a calendar year and award the winners, like Shane, with large cash prizes and the adoration of the surfing community the world over. By his own admission, though, he was quite lucky to be in the right place at the right time. The years that followed his retirement saw a massive surge in the growth of big wave surfing in a commercial sense, which was partly led by Shane himself.

Roaming the world in search of the biggest waves doesn't come, cheap and sponsors who were more than willing to help him rise to the challenge courted Shane, along with a handful of other guys for years. Even as little as ten years ago when a professional surfer retired, there weren't a whole lot of options to look forward to in order to pay the bills for the next thirty-odd years.

Big wave surfing has seen plenty of prestigious talents, but to be at the pinnacle of your career when the sport starts being recognised and blasted over main stream media is quite something else. While it would have been inconceivable years ago to make a living from such a specialist sport, Shane has effectively become the blueprint for what it takes to become a professional big wave surfer.

Shane grew up in a family that loved spending time at the beach. When he was three years old his family opened a beach restaurant called *Dorians*. As he was a little young to be waiting tables he found himself immersed in beach life from dawn till dusk, and it was here that he learned how to swim and surf. Although he started out on a body board, his father gifted him a surfboard for his fifth birthday and the rest, as they say, is history.

You would think, as an outsider looking in, that this prodigal son was nurtured from a young age by an over-zealous dad intent on making his son succeed and become the best, no matter what. Strangely, though, as Shane describes it, that wasn't the case and the father-son relationship was a little way away from what you might imagine, as he explains…

'My father was an alcoholic and pretty old school when it came to parenting. He left most of the responsibility of raising me up to my mom. He was never at the beach filming me and never at the surf contests that I entered, although I always wished he was. I loved him a lot and he was a good man, but I think a lot about him when I think about the kind of parent I want to be. He was always super supportive of my choice to become a professional surfer though. He led a fairly wild life and was at one time a stunt double for Elvis Presley. I guess not many sons can say that about their father. He was always very open to the different kind of lifestyle I wanted to pursue and often said that I had chosen the best way to meet a lot of beautiful women, which I always found kind of funny.'

That said, Shane is now married to Lisa, a native of California and a bikini-designer, and they are raising their two children – Jackson, who is twelve, and Charlie, who is nine. It was shortly after the birth of Jackson that Shane almost drowned while surfing at a spot called *Mavericks* in the chilly waters of Northern California. It was here, just shy of thirty miles north of San Francisco, that he met one of the most destructive and life-ending waves on the planet. Video footage of Shane's infamous wipe-out shows him turning to paddle for a wave in excess of forty feet. Then, when he is halfway through gliding down its steep face, he catches a ridge on the wave face and is propelled head first like a rag doll to the base of the wave before disappearing briefly and then being sucked over the falls. This basically means he is caught inside the body of the wave and becomes part of the pitching lip as it breaks into an avalanche of white water. If you watch it really closely you can see his head pop out the top as he goes over, which was just enough for him to take a vital breath. Otherwise, I suspect, he wouldn't have made it out alive. Spectators in the safety of the deep-water channel and on the beach wouldn't see any sign of Shane for nearly a minute. He was held under for so long by the first wave that he wasn't able to make it to the surface before another equally big wave roared through the line-up, holding him down and pushing him through the initial stages of blackout.

©Brian Bielmann

'After I fell, I was underwater and kept trying to swim up, but the wave kept pinning me down. I didn't have a chance to make any headway against the power of the wave. Just when it began to release me, the next wave was already on my head. So I never got a breath before the second wave hit and took me straight down to the reef. That's how a vast majority of people who have died surfing big waves drown. When you get held under for two waves your chances of survival are really, really low as death is a real possibility. I have had numerous close friends die surfing waves like this. It used to be that I never thought about it much but now I have a family and they are everything to me. I have to remember that they come first and I need to make responsible decisions so that I come home safely.'

Many a great surfer hasn't survived the ferocity of a two-wave hold-down. Some don't survive it physically, but many just never recover from the mental aspect of what it does to them, and these people are never the same person again. Coming that close to death and hearing its rattle has caused many a big wave surfer to re-evaluate his or her lifestyle. For his part Shane admits that the incident gave him a whole new perspective on life. While he was underwater he thought about his infant son and not being alive to see him grow up. He decided that what he was pursuing was simply too dangerous to continue on its present course. It was then that he came up with the idea of the inflatable vest and went on to pioneer the design with his major sponsor *Billabong*.

What it meant was that big wave surfers finally had their own version of a car airbag. These lightweight vests could be easily worn while surfing and should the surfer experience a bad wipe-out and be unable to get to the surface then all they needed to do was pull a cord, the vest would inflate and they would go shooting back up to the surface. Shane's original design won multiple awards for innovation. The vests are now starting to become commercially available and have become mandatory kit at most big wave events. Far from leaving only his legacy as one of the world's best big wave performers, Shane also leaves this life-saving vest that will hopefully save lives in the future.

Big wave surfing itself actually went through a bit of a makeover in the very late nineties and early millennium. Surfers began using jet skis to tow themselves into waves that were previously impossible to ride as they were too big to physically paddle into. This new-age approach to surfing really blew apart the big wave scene and suddenly anyone possessing a decent amount of skill and courage could ride a wave that wouldn't have been possible before. While Shane most certainly participated in the craze in its infancy, he laments that suddenly once empty surf spots were now buzzing with the sound of two stroke engines. Before the inception of the jet ski, if the biggest wave of the day rolled through a line-up of fifty surfers, maybe only three surfers really wanted that wave. With fifty guys being jet ski assisted you've got fifty guys who all want, and are capable of catching, that wave. That's not to say that towing is easy, it's just that it eliminates certain portions of the harder parts of surfing big waves ie being in the right position and having to use your own horsepower to catch them.

For Shane, these developments were a bit of a double-edged sword, as on the one hand they helped him ride bigger and crazier waves, but on the other hand they had levelled the playing field for others that he had previously dominated.

So what of this man, who is a global superstar in the world of surfing? We get a look behind the scenes through his Instagram feed – serving well over half a million followers – as he documents his surfing and life as a family man. How does a man raise young lives while risking his own from time to time?

'I see being a father as a huge responsibility and something you only get one shot at. I take it all pretty serious and try and be a good dad. I am grateful to have such a great wife and mother of my kids. Being parents is tough but I'm lucky to have such a solid partner to do it with.'

Given their children's love of surfing, might they both not one day wave goodbye to their children as they head off to surf the giant waves of Hawaii. To this he laughs.

'No, we haven't discussed that and I hadn't even thought of it till now. Both my kids love to surf and if they are interested in bigger waves as they get older then that's a decision that they have to make for themselves.'

His son, Jackson, is in fact something of a child prodigy on both a surfboard and a skateboard. He now has his own Instagram account where his unbelievable talents are showcased for all to see. In the last year Jackson has gone from just a kid, who looked like he had uncanny abilities for his age, to a young man who has started to look like he could possibly rival his father's abilities in a little over a decade's time. He's learning fast and is now sponsored by global brand *Billabong* just like his father. If you watch his videos, you'll soon see that it's not down to nepotism from Shane's sponsor or the fact that he carries the Dorian name, this young kid is the real deal!

Of Jackson's uncanny abilities at such a young age Shane explains with, I'd imagine a sparkle in his eyes, about his eldest child's attributes.

'Jackson has had athletic ability since he was very little. Even when climbing trees when he was a toddler, he would do it with skill and strength and awareness. He also has a capacity to overcome fear in many situations. Once when he was six he was watching me jump off a forty-five-foot cliff into a waterfall pond. He asked me to take him up there so he could see where I was jumping from. I thought nothing of it and on our way up he said, "I'm not walking back down, Dad, I am jumping". I thought once he saw the jump spot he would be terrified, but he said he really wanted to do it. I took some time to explain exactly what the dangers were and afterwards he didn't hesitate and jumped off. I was shocked, and pretty freaked out to be honest. That was when I had that initial thought like wow, this kid is not like most other kids.'

©Ryan Moss

So it seems the apple has in fact not fallen very far from the tree at all. Are we seeing the emergence of a young sporting superstar to match his father one day? Both their children are bright as buttons but you suspect that Jackson, like his father, has the lure of the ocean on his mind. You get a feeling that Shane is deeply involved with all aspects of his kids' lives, in a supportive way, and understands that childhood can be tough

In addition to surfing, Shane is a dedicated survivalist and is passionate about hunting in the wild. He's also very passionate about teaching his kids survival skills. Shane isn't your typical hunter and it was something that started becoming a way of life only a few years ago after he had moved out of town and into the wilds of his tropical island. He maintains that he actually has a problem with killing animals but says he eats meat himself, so whether it's him or someone else doing the killing really makes little difference. He says he only hunts for food his family can eat and only hunts animals that he likes to eat so you won't find any *taxidermy* elephants' heads adorning his walls. He sees it as a way to teach his kids how to survive in nature, in Hawaii, and give them a better understanding about the circle of life.

Every day when he is home, he and Jackson shoot arrows together. The young boy has become somewhat of his wingman on hunting trips. He says that some of his friends think it strange that he lets a twelve-year-old shoot a bow and arrow and handle a knife, but to Shane it would seem strange not to. He says this is the way boys should be raised and he teaches his son about respect for the wild and the consequences of being in it. The animals are real, he teaches him, and it's not a computer game. Nothing is wasted when they hunt and the meat is stored in the family freezer where it often finds its way into venison tacos that seem to be a family favourite. For Shane it's important that his son knows that when the arrow is still in the bow he is in control, but once it leaves his fingers nothing can be done to change the consequence of that action, and maybe that's the best piece of wisdom you could ever pass on to your children.

His youngest child, Charlie, is perhaps a little undecided on joining the boys on the hunt and busies herself with hobbies like photography and ballet. Although her mum, Lisa, says she very much enjoys the spoils of the hunt and knows exactly where it comes from. In this day and age when people are perhaps becoming less and less willing to accept the responsibility of their own actions, it's a breath of fresh air knowing that two kids in Hawaii know exactly where their food comes from. Shane also freely admits that he expects a lot from his children. He insists that they show respect and are kind to people, and he isn't afraid to tell them when he feels they are not.

It's pretty clear by watching the media document him, that he's not forcing his parenting choices down anyone's throat. Given that he is quite a prominent figure in the surfing world, he has, by sheer accident, found himself in the much sought-after role as a social influencer. For him, Hawaii is the perfect place to raise children and although it took his wife, Lisa, a little while to adapt from the fast-paced life of Los Angeles, they are now settled in Kona and very much enjoying the lifestyle it affords them. Shane explains how he teaches his kids about risk and danger. He says...

'I encourage them to take risks but only after knowing and understanding what the risks really are. Life is short and you never know what tomorrow will bring. I don't want my kids to live risky lives or be daredevils or anything like that. But I do encourage them to lead full lives and to put themselves out there when the reward is worth the risk.'

So how long can Shane remain at the top of his game? He explains that he needs to be in the best shape he can be but more for survival than anything else. Surfing big waves, as he says, is a mental game and if you don't feel confident being out there it adds a lot of danger to the situation. He regularly does a lot of breath-training and cardio intervals to strengthen his lung capacity.

Has he thought about what he would like to do when the day comes when he is no longer a paid sportsman? That, he says, will probably be working with children in some way, as he's really enjoyed coaching them at sporadic intervals throughout his career. Would he ever consider a return to the bright lights of Hollywood? (He starred in a surf film in the nineties called *In God's Hands*).

'I don't think so,' he said. 'But I'm glad I took that acting job when I was in my twenties on a film that was offered to me. The film itself was very embarrassing for me. I thought it was terrible and I was a horrible actor. But I do not regret doing it in the slightest. I chalk it up to a crazy little chapter in my life and a cool and unique opportunity and experience.'

At the moment he has a very full schedule, so Hollywood won't be required to pay the bills anytime soon. I wonder, though, if there are any common misconceptions the general public has about surfing.

'Oh, yes,' he said. 'That it is all perfect waves and good times. I am super grateful for my job and I would never complain about it but it does have its drawbacks. I have to be away from my family almost half the year and I know my kids wish I didn't have to be away from home so much. Many of the trips are away from the ocean doing promotional work for brands I am sponsored by. Having said that, I have no complaints and I manage it all very well with the support of my wife, Lisa.'

You get the distinct impression that if it were all to end tomorrow then Shane would be okay with that. He's already reached legendary status within his chosen profession and should remain there for a little while yet, one suspects. Shane is in optimum shape and if he's not getting worked over by his surf-mad kids dragging him to the beach then he's at the gym crunching weights. It's a good story about a very unassuming guy who takes a pretty fearless and unique approach to both his profession and his family life. Turns out though, his own dad was right, and that surfing was indeed a way to meet a beautiful girl which then led to a perfect little family of his own and possibly even a few more mini daredevils yet to come.

Given that his focus on big waves has never been contest-related you wonder what else he has left to achieve. He was asked a number of years ago before his kids were born about the prospect of paddling into a hundred-foot wave. He replied that he can't wait to give it a try if the opportunity ever presented itself. I wonder, given his now expanded family, does his desire to be the first to paddle into a wave that size still exist? To which he mimics his original answer from years before with an affirmative 'yes'. You get a lot of bravado in all sorts of sports but you know he means this when he says it. If he does find that elusive giant then you just know he's going to turn and go for it.

There's no looking back with this big wave legend.

"Monsters from the deep blue sea"

IV
THE FMX RIDER

It's theorised by many an individual in a white coat that as humans we only have a very small set of basic or innate emotions that we carry with us throughout our entire lifetime. Fear is one of those basic emotions that evolved with us since we first walked the Earth.

Fear itself is a very useful emotion to have as it's effectively the body's natural alarm bell that rings and tells us we need to take action, whether that's to run, freeze, hide or fight. Simply put, we would never have gotten as far as we did, had it not been for this marvellous invention of Mother Nature.

How does this aid to human survival actually work? Well, if you want to get into the neuroscience of it all then you need to understand a part of the brain called the amygdala. This extraordinary segment of the brain consists of two almond-shaped entities that are able to sense danger through what we see, and then quickly process that fear and notify the adjoining part of the brain. The reaction takes a mere nanosecond, which is quite helpful really, as the proverbial woolly mammoths can really rocket along once they get moving.

While the process of how fear envelops us is fairly clear, less is known about why it distributes itself in different degrees from one human to the next. All we know, with our limited understanding of the human brain, is that people experience fear in different ways and to different extremes. In today's modern world of extreme sports it seems that fear exists almost everywhere. Athletes routinely put their lives in danger by attempting stunts that seem to get more and more ludicrous while encouraged by armies of chanting fans.

If you've ever watched or had anything to do with an extreme sport then you will have heard the name Robbie Maddison. He is the quintessential modern-day stuntman. If death-defying jumps on a motorbike are what you want to see then he is most certainly your man, and by quite a margin. Through the course of his career in Freestyle Motocross (FMX) – in which competitors flip and fly through the air at obscene heights and speeds – Robbie has won just about everything worth winning and broken a whole stack of world records along the way.

While Robbie competed in FMX for many years, in the later part of his career he successfully specialised in one-off stunts to thrill audiences around the world. For those feats Robbie is routinely described as the modern-day Evel Knievel – a title that's certainly not just given to anyone.

The thrill-seeking bug bit Robbie at a very young age – he'd had a BMX bike from almost since he could walk. However, pedal power was never going to be enough for this young man, and he fell in love with the idea of riding a motorbike at the age of three when he would watch little kids riding bikes on television. He also had a young neighbour who would ride past the house on his bike almost daily. He recalls running up to the window and staring, mouth wide open, wishing for a motorbike all of his own.

'It's funny to think back to that time as I had only recently learned to speak but I clearly remember asking Santa for one thing the following Christmas – and that was for a motorbike. I wanted to be certain he knew what I wanted so I didn't want to confuse the big guy with any multiple present requests.'

Thankfully Santa got the message and that shiny new petrol-powered bike under the tree is where it all started for him. He gets asked now and then if there was a moment when he realised he had a gift for riding. While he isn't sure, he does say he remembers never getting sick of riding any of his bikes, whether that was a BMX or a motorbike. He was virtually glued to both almost every day, and usually all day, spending much more time at it than the other kids. He became better, faster, and gained greater confidence. He soon began to do things that other kids the same age just wouldn't consider.

He describes himself as being very tunnel-visioned with almost everything he did, whether learning to whistle, juggle, or ride a unicycle, swimming, surfing or skating. No matter the activity, once he decided he wanted to learn it, that was it, and he'd stick to it until he'd figured it out, without any hint of frustration. A lightbulb moment in his head was when he made the full-time transition from a BMX to a motor bike. Even back then he was adamant it was what he wanted to do with the rest of his life, which is quite bizarre considering at the time he was knee high to a grasshopper, as they say in his native Australia.

'Every day I would take my shovel and go and build bigger and harder jumps to ride off. I never had any idea at that age where I was going to end up, but it was all I ever wanted to do.'

His first major taste of success came in the new and emerging sport of Freestyle Motocross. Its progression into the hugely popular sport it's now become began back in the early nineties. Robbie often says that he believes that you're always in the right place at the right time, and that was very true for him.

To be his age when it was all taking off put him in pole position to take the sport anywhere he wanted to take it.

FMX is an extremely dangerous sport. The sheer power of the bikes the competitors ride, and the heights and speeds they reach, make even the seemingly routine just a little deadly. Typical FMX competitions are run in stadiums around courses with multiple jumps, and the rider is judged on the execution and difficulty of their run. It's now gotten to the point where competitors completely let go of the bike mid-air and they almost fly alongside it like Superman, which is exactly who the trick is named after.

It was the evolution of the backflip, though, that really changed the course of the sport. The first person to try this on a full-size bike was the American, Carey Hart, back in 2000. These FMX guys are rock stars in their own right – Carey is married to the singer Pink – and command full stadiums wherever they ride. It was around this time that a young Robbie was just starting to be noticed. His break-out year came in 2004 when he won a gold medal at the Planet X Games, which was held in his home country of Australia. His trip to the top of the podium involved completing thirteen backflips in a row, which was enough to beat the headline riders of the event. He jokes that the next day his phone nearly went into meltdown with all the requests to book him for future events.

You would have thought, back then, at the relatively young age of twenty-five, his career plan would have sent him down the familiar path of travelling the world on the FMX circuit for the next decade, pushing the limits and chancing his luck with however many broken bones he could sustain until he was no longer able to ride. But this is where the story of Robbie Maddison's life gets a bit weird, and suggests that perhaps the aforementioned amygdala function of his brain just isn't sending out the same doses of fear that other brains do.

You see, choosing the path of a full-time FMX rider would have actually been a safer bet mortality-wise compared to what he ended up choosing, which was to follow his idol, Evel Knievel, and reinvent the world of stunt jumping.

There is of course, no comparison, as he says, between himself and the greatest stunt rider of all time. The difference in equipment and technology back then compared to the present day is like a different universe, and the bikes that people ride today make it possible to go faster and jump further. While there is truth in that comparison for sure, he's also obviously being very modest. It really comes down to the mindset of the individual more than anything else, and in that the two men are very much alike. Robbie loves the buzz that Evel was able to create around his jumps, and that is definitely something he tries to emulate.

'When Evel jumped, the world knew about it,' he says, 'and that's the same kind of energy and excitement I want to have before I take my jumps.'

Before I get to the stunts which have somewhat defined his career, it's worth mentioning the carnage that he's put his body through in order to get to where he is today. Once you know the horrors he has inflicted upon himself, it only makes the things he has done seem even more incredible. There's the broken neck, the collar bones which have both been snapped several times each, two broken legs, a brain haemorrhage, a punctured lung, a ruptured scrotum, snapped anterior cruciate ligaments, fractured vertebrae, multiple lesser fractures, spinal injuries, numerous concussions and a torn lower lip. He's had his front teeth knocked out and replaced and his nose broken a dozen times. He's dislocated the same shoulder four times in five days during a multimillion-dollar shoot for his sponsors, but he carried on and completed it with a half-functioning arm. Then there was the time his heart stopped beating from a heavy crash-landing. And that's without even mentioning the time that he almost drowned. In case you are wondering, yes, he was on his bike when that happened, but that comes later in the chapter.

'My heart has stopped beating many times from traumatic injury so I've been as close to death as anyone has been on many occasions. I'm certainly lucky to still be here today and it's a miracle, to be honest, that I can still walk and talk.'

Robbie has had so many injuries and so many surgeries that he was the personification of a human piñata considering all the beatings he has taken. He was also at one point held together with so many steel pins that it's a wonder he was ever able to pass through airport security. He has now had all the hardware removed from his body because, he says, if he were to crash with metal in a bone and break that same bone again, it would shatter, making it virtually impossible for surgeons to fix.

I start to wonder how he was ever able to ride in the first place given all the tears and breakages, not to mention how one can recover from the pain and still want to do it all over again.

Robbie's entry into the world of stunt jumps started back in 2005, and through to 2009 he attempted to break world records for long-distance jumping. During this period there were three record-breaking jumps and every single time he bettered his last jump. Huge amounts of time, energy and money go into making these types of spectacles happen, and the logistics of building these huge jumps takes an army of bulldozers days to create. I'm fairly certain that one has to be a different kind of rider to be able to function under that much pressure.

With standard FMX competitions there is always the danger of serious injury. Although deaths do occur, thankfully these numbers remain small. With the stunt jumps Robbie was doing, death was probably a more realistic outcome than injury, such was the magnitude of what he was doing. The distances he was travelling were well over one hundred metres, which is not far off the length of a football pitch. Add to the fact that he is also twenty metres in the air and you have on your hands the potential for some very serious consequences. The speed at which he travels is probably one of the hardest things to comprehend as he's literally a blur as he hits the ramp. It's all super calculated though, as even 5mph can make a massive difference. You have to wonder what on earth goes through his head when he's heading full throttle towards the ramp.

'Fear and confidence work in relation to each other, so a big part of being fearless is having confidence. Confidence in one's ability is something you can't fake; you get it from your experience that you have built up in your preparation and in previous jumps. In a way it evolves through trial and error and knowing exactly how to handle yourself in any given situation. Once I work up to a certain level of confidence I keep my head clear; clear of any negativity, doubt or superstitions. When you've been there and seen friends seriously injured, it's always there in the back of your mind but it has to be blocked out. Finally, once I'm sure all is in order, I just stay confident. I don't let fear even surface. Whenever it tries to register I just shut it down, take a deep breath and be at one with my jump.'

It comes as no surprise to discover that Robbie is actually one of the best-known Australian sports personalities in the USA. That's quite an achievement for a boy from the very sleepy coastal town of Kiama in New South Wales. That success for Robbie doesn't come without partnerships, and he'd be nowhere near where he is today without the support of his sponsors – *Red Bull* and *DC Shoes* – both of which back him with financial support.

Robbie also has another partner in crime: his wife, Amy, whom he has been with since 2004. She is almost as much of a feature of his jumps as he is, and is always pictured nervously awaiting the outcome. She looks every inch the quintessential Australian girl – blonde, bubbly and beautiful; everything Australia's women are famous for. She is also a dab hand at running a business, he says, and is behind the scenes making sure everything runs smoothly. If there was an X Games gold medal for worry and anxiety, Amy would win it. She's seen enough carnage on the track to last a lifetime.

Robbie and Amy met in a somewhat unique way in that Robbie became good friends with Amy's brother and father well before he ever met her. Her brother was a world champion wakeboarder at the time so they crossed paths and did a few TV interviews together. Robbie eventually met Amy at an event in her home town, and they immediately hit it off. Though he never mentions it, I suspect an extra ticket to the event would have been purchased for her by the family so that she could meet the young man whom she would eventually go on to marry.

I joke with him that it's probably the closest thing to an arranged marriage that the two families have ever seen. He is, as you would expect, glowing in the praise he heaps on her and not just because of the three sons she has given him. They are, as he puts it, a dynamic duo. She organises his life behind the scenes, making sure everything from insurance to hotel bookings are sorted and that he is packed correctly for trips. It's not easy to organise three small kids (and a large one) for overseas travel but she takes it all in her stride. Incidentally, They never discussed the dangers of his job before they had kids as Amy accepted that riding was just what he did and will hopefully always do.

So how exactly does one of the world's most famous daredevils raise children? Well, he and Amy have certainly got their hands full with Kruz, who is eight, Jagger, who is five and with their newest arrival, Rocco, who is a year old. The older boys really are a chip off the old block and are mad keen bikers as well. The boys have travelled all over the world since they were babies to see their dad perform so it's all they really know, and it's only a matter of time before the baby of the family dons a helmet.

Robbie says that he has no time to waste worrying about the future when tomorrow is never promised. He isn't totally sold on his kids riding bikes as a career as he knows that it's a very hard road. What's more, it would be almost impossible to recreate what he has done. He ran the gauntlet and was at the right place at the right time, but only time will tell with the boys.

He has no regrets about taking those risks and making the most of the latter part of his career. The family are now financially stable and he can spend a lot more time with them as his career winds down. However, he is keen to point out he has a few more dreams he wants to realise, and then, maybe, it will be time to retire.

Oh, and what dreams they have been so far for this stuntman who knows no limitations. In January 2009, live, and in front of a world audience, Robbie jumped ninety-six feet from a small ramp up onto the top of a replica Arc de Triomphe – two thirds of the original size – in Las Vegas. The jump was extraordinary as it was almost a sheer vertical leap. He landed on top perfectly, but that was the easy part, he tells me. To reach the safety of the ground he had to effectively drive his motorbike off a cliff face, back down to a ramp that started fifty feet below. He very slightly overshot the ramp and landed a little lower on the transition of the ramp than was ideal, but it was still a very clean landing and goes to show the skill you need to control the bikes when things don't go perfectly. Such was the force of the landing that it tore the webbing on his hand to the bone, but it was a small price to pay for what he says, right up until 2017, has been the biggest highlight of his riding career.

The really intriguing part of the stunt was that it was made up of two very distinct parts – the climb and the descent – and they were separated by a few minutes, which gave him time to think. For the most part, extreme sports don't have that kind of intermission as they are foot to the floor from start to finish. Not only did he have to recover from the huge adrenaline rush of making it to the top but he actually had to control that rush of emotions, and properly assess his chances of making it back down by peering over the edge. The psychological part of the stunt has really never been explored before, but it says boundless things about his physical make-up. I think most people would have been happy enough to make it to the top and quit while they were ahead. Robbie exhibited remarkable mental skill by being able to go from high to low, to high again, all the while aware that his every move was being watched by millions of people all over the world. However you want to argue about what sets people apart from others, there is no denying that some of us possess slightly more animalistic portions of the basic survival instincts that humans were meant to have.

It was around this point, just a few months after this stunt, that he came to a bit of a crossroads in his career. He was doing his big stunts but still trying to do his best at FMX competitions. You get the feeling he had to prove to the other riders, and to himself, that he wasn't just a stunt rider with a foot either side of the fence. So, with a torn hand only just recently mended and with probably not the best pre-event preparation, he took on the best riders in the world at the Red Bull X-Fighters' competition in Alberta, Canada and won. While he didn't quite come out of the mist, so to speak, he still beat the best of the best, head to head. It was truly remarkable, not because he wasn't up to the challenge, but because he wasn't as match fit as his competitors were and because his attention had been divided between stunts and competitions.

The win proved quite the catalyst for a new dawn in his career and some death-defying jumps. You might assume that the ideas for these stunts come from his sponsors or public relations team keen to raise his profile, but in fact they all come from his own imagination. He carries with him a small sketch book in which he draws out ideas for stunts and then attempts to make them happen. When we get into some of those recent stunts that started out as sketches you can seriously imagine family and friends getting the shakes anytime they see him face down, sketching away.

He now definitely works harder than he ever did before but often feels like he's drowning in his own ideas and all the work they create. However, he insists the struggle is worth it because if it were easy everyone would be doing it. He very much enjoys being at the forefront of something and leading the way.

The years from 2009 until 2011 continued to see a number of incredible stunts. He completed a back flip on Tower Bridge in London when the drawbridges were twenty-five feet apart. He jumped the Corinth canal in Greece, and while the jump itself was only eighty metres in distance, which is quite short compared to his typical jumps, it was more about the danger of not making it. Of all his jumps, he thinks that one potentially had the highest consequences in terms of him becoming a fatality, given that the valley of the canal was so steep and with a sheer rock cliff at either side. Having survived this, he went on to jump across San Diego bay in tandem with a snow mobile rider on a specially made run-up and ramp of quite massive proportions. The goal was to hit the four-hundred-foot mark for the jump. In the end, the snowmobile made the mark but Robbie missed it by a few feet.

As he reflects on his feats, Robbie is very gracious about both his mother and father, who were very supportive of his career. He was most fortunate that they were in a position to fund his love of riding when he was developing his skills before the sponsorship dollar arrived on the scene. His own upbringing, and his relationship with his father, was also very important, especially now he has three children of his own.

'I think as fathers we always try to do things our own way. My dad showed me I needed to raise my boys with some discipline by raising me with it himself. I, of course, hated it at the time, but it made me who I am today and taught me valuable lessons on how to raise my own children. My boys aren't allowed to just run wild; they follow the rules or else they sit in their rooms or get isolated from using the things they love. They are very, very good kids, and I love them for their spirit, but both Amy and I know we have to keep that wild side in check.'

He admits that times have changed from when he was a child and the world seems a more complicated and scary place than he recalls. Every day the world becomes more populated and the stakes go up for him. He feels strongly about educating his children about the realities of life and about making sure that his kids know the difference between right and wrong.

©Garth Milan

Robbie's latest stunt, in which he attempted to ride a wave in the ocean on a specially adapted bike, was truly ground-breaking and certainly a spectacle to watch. The idea was the culmination of two years' hard work, testing and planning, and he only had a window of two weeks to film the stunt after having had no actual practice in the ocean. Robbie and the team chose Tahiti for the shoot and a wave called *Teahupoo*, which is one of the deadliest waves on Earth as it can reach heights of around seven metres over a razor-sharp coral reef. It took several years to develop the technology to make the stunt possible, and the bike had to be specially adapted for it. In the end, though, it came down to trial and error, and although he was able to actually plane across a few waves, the bike ended up underwater for a good amount of time.

Seeing a dirt bike riding a wave with all the local surfers scrambling to get out of the way was quite a sight to behold. Obviously, motorcycles and salt water don't mix terribly well, so there was a painstaking amount of repairs that needed to be made every time the bike went underwater.

As the team was finally in a position to shoot the scene of Robbie riding the bike on a large wave, there was a fresh storm brewing in the South Pacific Ocean and rapidly approaching Tahiti. The launch itself took place off a pontoon on a bike that was fitted with a foil under it that looked a bit like a giant water ski. The wave, however, is hard to navigate, and the reason things well in the early attempts is that he and his team had expert advice from local riders on jet skis. However, as the waves became bigger, the supervising skiers decided that it was safer if they were further in to the shore to make any potential rescue easier.

Robbie was essentially left alone on the pontoon to make his own decision about what wave to catch and in the end he made, by his own admission, a very bad call. He rode off the pontoon and into an almost four-metre wave. He did manage to ride it for a few seconds, which was spectacular, but in the end the wave outran him and he was forced to aim for the beach to outrun it. Unfortunately, he had no chance against the avalanche of white water behind him and he was engulfed. The beating he received was worsened by the fact that his full riding gear left him quite restricted underwater.

Robbie is adamant that it was only his ten or so years of surfing experience that saved him from drowning. He's fairly specific about the moment he was on the bike and knew that there was no way he was going to be able to outrun it. He tells me he took the biggest, deepest breath he had ever taken and waited for the ocean to unleash its fury on him. The thing about the ocean is that waves don't come in ones, like jumps, so surviving the first wave just meant a second one was on its way.

'It felt like I was a rag doll in a washing machine and I was really, really struggling for breath, especially still having my helmet on. I sort of had a sixth sense of intuition at one point that I was near the surface and I managed to get my head above water and take a quick breath before the next wave hit me. Had I not got that air, I feel I would have drowned; there was no two ways about it. I had a sickening feeling that I was never going to see Amy and the boys again and that rocked me pretty hard. I still feel like I accomplished something, though, and achieved what I set out to do. So, for that part I'm happy with the whole experience but feel incredibly lucky to be alive.'

Some time has now elapsed since the heroics of Tahiti, and since then Robbie has by his own standards been lying a little dormant. The thing is that the stunts he does sometimes take years of planning to fulfil, and I expect hidden away in that little sketch book of dreams is something that is going to rock the stunt world to its core.

I suggest, jokingly, that maybe he could backflip out of a Hercules plane from nine thousand feet and parachute to the ground and then ride out the landing... There is something of a pause at the other end of the line and then laughter. Does that mean he's considering it? How cool would that be, I think to myself, knowing that I've probably just been crossed off Mrs Maddison's Christmas card list forever. One thing is for sure: deep down he's still that little kid with a shovel in his back yard, building jumps and dreaming of the impossible; only now the shovel is a bulldozer and the dreams are a whole lot bigger.

"Full throttle thrills and spills"

V
THE ULTIMATE FIGHTER

©Scottya

Seldom do I imagine that chances like this come along very often: the opportunity to write about a person who is a world champion whom I have known almost since birth seems fairly unlikely but that's just the position I find myself in with this chapter. It is incredibly hard to become a world champion of anything these days, especially in fighting sports given the high level of participation that has resulted from them becoming popular television sports. What makes it better is that it's a small town hero kind of story as you don't get too many world champions from the tiny Australian island of Tasmania. Tasmania, as they say, is about as far away from anywhere as you can get, and no statement could be truer.

The subject of this chapter, Shannon King, had a fairly typical upbringing. The son of a saw-mill manager, he lived with his mother, father and siblings in a modest house in the small coastal town of Wynyard. He was a wiry little kid but gifted with that extra portion of coordination and a boundless amount of energy. As the young boy grew out of his wiry frame and freckles, he suddenly found himself a lot taller and broader than anyone might have expected him to become – with the kind of physique that lends itself to excelling in almost anything. I've been told by people that had a sport association with him over the years that he could have done just about anything he wanted and been outstanding at it. In the end he chose martial arts and then boxing and took them both just about as far as they could go.

He's been a professional fighter and world champion but finally hung up his boots a year ago. By doing so he brought the curtain down on his stellar career in which he fought over fifty professional fights across two separate disciplines. He's dished out some stunning blows to his opponents in that time but also received a few as well. Part of being a good champion is knowing when your time is up and still being able to walk, if not hobble, out of the ring, as opposed to exiting on a stretcher.

The start of his career began back in 2003 when he took up Muay Thai – also known as Thai boxing – when he was twenty-five years old. Muay Thai is an extremely deadly form of martial art and is often referred to as *the art of eight limbs* because it is characterised by the combined use of fists, elbows, knees and shins. The whole body becomes a fighting unit which coordinates itself in order to search for its opponent's weaknesses. The world of Muay Thai is extraordinarily difficult to excel in as it is an increasingly crowded and competitive market place with a high calibre of the fighters.

Thai fighters have hardened bones through their training and don't feel pain like ordinary people. While it's not a well-known fact, humans can actually harden and increase the density of their bones the more they hit harder objects with them. Receiving a kick to the body from a top-tier fighter can cause extreme damage to the body.

Shannon was so good at the sport that he fought on some of the biggest promotional tickets in Thailand while he was at the peak of his powers, which is saying something as Thai fighters tend to dominate the billboards and posters.

Shannon confirms that there are actually physical differences between Muay Thai fighters from Thailand and ones from other parts of the world. Thai fighters start very young, sometimes as early as eight years old. For this reason they have had, by the time they reach their peak, considerably more fights than foreign opponents and their bones are much harder.

While Shannon may have fought eight times a year, Thai fighters can fight twice a week. Some of the fighters from Thailand he works with at his gym sometimes shy away from fighting other Thais, preferring the 'wooden' legs white people have, when compared to the 'metal' ones of their fellow countrymen.

There is considerable discipline involved in training, especially when it comes to preparations for an upcoming fight. Diet, he says, is a huge discipline because of the mathematically calculated menus and strict intake of foods. 'It's not the one hour inside the ring that's important; it's what you do with the twenty-three hours outside the ring that count.' In fact, the diet is so strenuous that it is one of the major reasons that people decide to retire.

Shannon's pre-fight condition is something to behold. There are no boxes left unticked and the muscle tone has an etched-in-stone like appearance. So low is his body fat at his peak that his skin almost appears to have been drawn tight around its shell. You'd probably have trouble finding a piece of skin loose enough to grab even with a set of pliers. The fitness levels are also off the chart. He describes himself pre-fight as being stupidly fit. This help, he says, when it comes to doing things with the kids, as he has so much more energy. In fact, he believes it's a dad's responsibility to stay fit and healthy in order to be active with the kids.

Strangely, Shannon doesn't find his sport dangerous although he admits it can cause some deaths, as indeed boxing does. He says that he finds sports like football more dangerous as you have people coming at you from all angles. With Muay Thai every danger is there, directly in front of you, and all you have to do is be well enough trained to deal with it. It makes sense in a way, but I'm sure most people would choose a game of football over a round in the ring with him or any other Thai fighters.

Shannon has some incredible tales of bouts where he has won against all odds, including a fight in which his opponent actually burst one of Shannon's eardrums with a heavy blow to the head in the third round. It was, he says, incredibly painful and also affected his equilibrium which you really don't want to mess with. Despite this he fought on through another six rounds. So focused was he that he was able to manage the pain and in the end was actually able to knock the other guy out in the ninth round. Video footage of the event shows the crowd going crazy and his trainers looked like they were going to lose their minds. However, that's when the adrenaline really started to course through him and he totally forgot about his burst ear drum. Next day though, the surgeon brought him back down to earth when he properly diagnosed it.

Ever since that fight he developed a lot more self-belief as he knew he could carry himself through some pretty tough moments and still come out on top. However, there are always moments, he says, when you stare across the ring at your opponent and think there is no way you can beat them. He's had that feeling plenty of times, thinking the other guy was just too fast or had a better skill set. The thing is, he says, that after a few minutes you start to realise they are human too, and that's when you relax your fears and get busy trying to find a way to knock him to the floor.

Some of the misconceptions that people have about professional fighters – that they are *thugs*, for example – do annoy him as he considers himself an athlete simply looking to beat his opponent as other athletes do.

I can't help asking Shannon why he started in the fighting arts and whether it had anything to do with bullying. This wasn't the impetus for him but he does admit it may have started as a seed in his mind from the rough and tumble of the playground and standard younger sibling type stuff. It certainly never had anything malicious about it. He states that he learned a lot from his dad, who was a great role model and a very fair person. He recalls many times during his youth when his dad would stick up for people and encourage him and his two younger brothers and sister to do the same for people at school who were being targeted by bullies. He now finds himself doing the same with his girls and encouraging them to do the same thing at school. Perhaps, he says, the behaviour he learned from his father somehow ingrained something in his psyche about self-defence, but he isn't totally sure. He says he thinks the reason he stuck with the sport is that the whole discipline just clicked with him. It was probably equally likely that it was because he was so good at it.

Shannon is, above all things, an extremely proud father and husband. He is married to a very smart and beautiful lady called Natalie. A lawyer, she looks like she has walked straight out of a modelling catalogue. Between the two of them they managed to create two very bright and beautiful girls called Jessica Jordan and Alicia and who are eleven and twelve respectively. His wife has always been hugely supportive; she always encouraged him to continue with his passion and never put any pressure on him to roll back his career to find a safer one after they had children. She is, though, he says with a wry smile, somewhat of a fiery lady and their eldest daughter, Alicia, has also inherited that spark. On occasion when he feels a bit overwhelmed with the girls "opinions" as he kindly puts it, he takes refuge with his youngest daughter, Jessica Jordan, who is a very much more chilled-out character like him, and he bides his time with her until the dust settles.

He also tells me that he has never shied away from letting his daughters watch him fight, even from an early age. While it might certainly raise eyebrows with some people, Shannon has let his girls watch him fight for as long as he can remember. His eldest, Alicia, has watched him get knocked to the ground twice in his last-ever fight before he retired. Jessica, however, on this occasion was under the table fast asleep, exhausted from her day's activities. It's always hard to decide as a parent what to expose your children to, and what to shield them from, but at the end of the day you're preparing them for the real world and that's his motto. He and his wife have always ascribed to the theory that so long as things are explained to them properly beforehand, in most cases they let them witness the highs and lows of his career.

'I think I've always let the girls know that it's a good sport and I always gave my all, every time. So I think this lesson was more important than the risk of them seeing me get hurt. In a way, I guess, I parent by actions, not words, and I hope they take that resolve into their later lives when they are grown up and we aren't there to watch over them every second of the day.'

He often gets asked if his perspective on life and career changed much after he had children. To a certain extent he admits that it did, but he still wanted to continue with his path in life just in the safest way possible, which really meant becoming as good at it as he could, as he was his own protector. He tells me bluntly that he's a big advocate of the view that life changes for the better after kids, especially one's attitude towards safety.

'It's a special moment when my littlest one writes me cards wishing me luck in fights which is the total opposite of my eldest who just wants me to win.'

And there have certainly been no shortage of wins. I asked him if he thinks there was anything that gave him the edge over others he fought. He says for him personally, he thinks it's because he never *sooked* when something wasn't going his way. *Sooked*, I might add, is a very Australian term, and means not to whinge or complain.

He explains it like never complaining when the going gets tough, which happened plenty of times when he would come back to the corner of the ring after a rare beating or when he was frustrated at not being able to get around an opponent's defence. His reply to his trainer who asked how he was, was always 'I'm good. I'm ready', even if he wasn't really feeling like he was.

Shannon says that he has only really been scared once in the ring when competing in Muay Thai. He'd flown all the way to compete in Japan against a fighter from Thailand, so it was a pretty big deal. It was also the year before he won his world title. For whatever reason his defence failed him at the start and the guy's first kick hit him square on the thigh.

'It was like nothing I'd ever felt before and I was in so much pain that I was sure my leg was broken. I mean, I've felt pain like you wouldn't believe, but this was on a whole other level. I tried to keep my composure and dodge his onslaught while I worked out if my leg was broken.'

Luckily all bones were intact and he gradually came around and when the bell went he was very relieved to take respite in his corner to get himself together. Not being one to mince words he's ashamed to say that at the time he was pretty scared and didn't know how on earth he was going to get through the fight. It's a good example of Shannon's self-belief and inner strength and how he's managed to achieve what he has. He kept thinking to himself... 'You've come all this way. Don't finish in the second round.' He lied when his trainer asked how he was and said 'good', then promptly got up and continued the fight.

He's proud to say he actually ended up having what he believes was the best fight of his career as he had to fight so smart against a guy who clearly intimidated him. While he didn't win the match, he only lost by a very narrow points' margin, which was a pretty incredible result considering the opening round.

We have a brief chat about the kinds of insurances he had in case something did go wrong in the ring. Any kind of fighting and especially boxing is incredibly hard to get accident cover for. This adds to the risk factor quite a lot as you can be on your own in certain instances if something does go wrong in the ring and you're seriously injured. He adds this is why he was so frenetic in many ways with the business side of things.

He was lucky to have a great mentor who advised him early on about the best way to invest for the future. He effectively had to write his own insurance contract to make sure he could support his family in all eventuating circumstances. He did the right thing and listened to that advice, which is why he is in the position he is in now, he says. They will all be well looked after should something happen. Even though he is now retired he's smart enough to know that certain conditions in fighting sports can remain hidden for years, especially those that relate to brain trauma.

Shannon has been very successful both in life and business but he does have some regrets. By his own admission, he has always tried to do too many things at once. This was especially prevalent during his younger years when he was unable to resist the temptation to do multiple sports. While he did well at many, it might have been this all-in approach that robbed him of the chance to excel at just one sport earlier on. Even now I remind him that he's still unable to focus on only one fighting discipline in that he competed in both Muay Thai and boxing at the same time, something that's rarer than you might think.

Becoming an Australian boxing champion three times over was a big career highlight for him and he held the title in the 70 kg junior middleweight division. His last big fight in boxing was a nationally televised affair that actually broke the viewer record for the most watched boxing match in Australia. He says that he didn't find the transition from Muay Thai too difficult and it wasn't as if he had to constantly remember that he couldn't use his legs to kick. It was almost the exact opposite and he was glad to give his legs a break from a decade's hard impacts.

Interestingly for those who like facts, fighters may not have anything at all to eat or drink for up to thirty-six hours before a pre-fight weigh-in for boxing in order to make sure they are the correct weight to qualify for the fight. Depriving the body of food and water for that long can do strange things to the mind and cause the person to become confused and erratic and for this reason it's not uncommon for fights to break out – hence the security at these events. Fight don't always break out because the fighters dislike each other, although I'm sure that plays a part too.

Shannon also has itchy feet in the business world, with a very successful chain of gyms in his home state of Queensland, Australia. He laments that everything up to this point in his life has been done at a very frenetic pace and there has barely been time to stop and appreciate his achievements, but he is trying to a bit more now. He also now has more time to spend with his family which he's making the most of.

There are some funny tales from his heyday about the celebrity status that he used to enjoy in his home city of Brisbane. Apparently, as the tale goes, he was greeted by many as simply the "champ". You do see that kind of stuff in *Rocky* movies but it actually happened to him in real life. He is a very modest guy so I'm sure he took it all in his stride, but I'm sure he was smiling to himself deep down.

As we get on to the subject of self-defence, I ask about his thoughts on violence in public with the growing number of assaults as well as home invasions in big cities. It's interesting to ask Shannon about the safety of his family as I tell him that men often worry quite a lot about this kind of thing. He admits that if he was to experience a situation in public that endangered his family then he feels confident he would be able to deal with it perhaps better than most. He's never had to so far though, luckily, and says that he always keeps a sharp eye out for any behaviour that looks suspicious, alluding to the fact that he is very protective of his three ladies, outside and inside the home.

'Being a professional fighter you are constantly in control of your emotions. You're so focused on the job of winning the fight that you simply see your opponent as an obstacle. I don't fear them and I don't hate them. Winning is all I care about. If you or he is injured along the way then so be it, you both signed an open contract the moment you stepped in the ring together. I could get in trouble here because I believe a home should be off limits to any criminal. A home is where a kid should feel safe, one hundred percent of the time. For someone to take that away from them, possibly for life, I don't really want to write what I would do to them.'

Shannon isn't really one for handing out advice to people but he's proud of the way he's raised his girls. Of course there are some regrets that his schedule wasn't always as child-friendly as it could have been. That is just the reality of modern life and of being the main breadwinner. He and his wife have raised Alicia and Jessica to be able to handle the real world and not to complain about how unfair things can be sometimes. He knows life can be really unfair for some people and that it's the job of parents to make sure their kids are well equipped to handle their share of ups and downs.

Speaking of ups and downs he's definitely having a few of his own lately in trying to come to terms with his own retirement. In boxing especially, there is a long list of ex-champions who have had some troubled times after they left the ring, often drugs, alcohol or violence related. They are chasing the high they get from fighting, which in his opinion is totally unattainable with anything but fighting. While teetotal himself he still finds it difficult at the moment knowing he won't step into the ring again. He's also very honest and says that maybe he misses the recognition.

'When you win fights against all odds and you feel the adulation from the crowd, there really isn't anything like it. All the hard work and sacrifices are instantly forgotten and you are blown away from what has just happened.'

Now that he's retired he admits that he can feel a bit lost at times, and finds himself questioning what life is all about and that it's important to find a new path in life to bring him some individual fulfilment. He knows that it will turn around but it just takes time to adjust and be comfortable, but that will be the case eventually.

'I always parented by example with the girls and my fighting was a big part of that. I find now that I have difficulty in trying to explain things to them where, before, I would show them what you could do by achieving things myself and have them look on.'

That said, he's a smart guy and knows he is a lucky man to have such a family and that's super important to him.

He has a pretty positive outlook on life. His girls are growing up fast and will soon be making their own way in the world. He says he believes in human beings as a whole; thinks we will do the right thing to look after the world. He thinks if we concentrate on making our kids the kind of people we want them to be then we will be fine. It's refreshing in a way to hear such an opinion in these days of doom and gloom.

Although it's a bit clichéd I ask him about what is going to happen when his two gorgeous girls start having male suitors come a-calling at the front door. I can't quite decipher from his reply whether he is serious or joking, but he says that any young man wishing to take his daughter out on a date will get a leisurely tour through his extensive trophy room and a detailed explanation of what being a Muay Thai and boxing champion means to him. For extra effect he has compiled a short film of his greatest fights and that will be playing on three large screens around the room. I know he's not being totally serious but I do feel for the young men who will surely attempt to take his daughters out on dates.

"Kicks that break bones"

VI
THE BOMB DISPOSAL TECHNICIAN

As far as careers go in terms of not being family-friendly, working with highly problematic explosive devices has got to be right at the top of the list. Children typically prefer two parents instead of one, or at least two with fully functioning limbs, but TNT doesn't really distinguish between wants and needs and therein lies the problem.

Perhaps it's a misguided notion but it seemed as if people involved in this work might not really be the kind of people who would want families. One could assume they'd accepted that they could be blown up at any time so it probably wasn't wise to speculate on family life. Surprisingly that isn't the case, and they go about their careers and family lives just like anyone else, although I suspect just a little more carefully than most.

These guys certainly do not grow on trees and it was, you could say, a fairly arduous task to locate one that would work well in terms of the book's concept. Even once such a person was sourced there was still the issue of extracting the information from him, and that's tough because they have extraordinarily busy schedules. A lapse of five months occurred between initial contact and the actual interview itself. As a civilian, it sort of left me on tenterhooks as every day, without closure, meant another day he could possibly be blown to pieces, and then the search for a new candidate would have to begin again.

As an amusing side note the interview took place on speakerphone in my house, in full earshot of my own family. At one point I'm invited out to the workshop to have a look around at all the bomb devices as an educational exercise. Looking over at my wife she glances at me with an expression that says... *You have two young children and you're not going anywhere near any bomb, defuzed or otherwise. If you do, the locks will be changed when you return...*

Colin King is fifty-six years old and is a resident of the United Kingdom. You could most certainly call him a bomb disposal "expert", but that part of his title seems a little incongruous. After all, can you really work with bombs and be anything less than an expert? Colin runs his own bomb disposal company and travels all over the world as a hired gun, defuzing all manner of explosive devices along the way. He's vastly experienced and is often called upon by top-tier government and private enterprise agencies to give his opinion on all things explosive. Every year he spends in his job means he instantly becomes more respected than the previous year. Essentially that means the longer he lives the better he gets at what he does.

How do you get into a lifestyle of explosives? After all, it's not your average job, and it's certainly not for your average person. The natural assumption is that you'd expect to get some tale of joining the military and then perhaps moving divisions for a military life full of action and adventure. As it turns out that was a way off reality although, yes, he did in fact join the army in bomb disposal in 1986. It turns out that from the age of ten a young Colin was already busy making explosives and bombs and he was reading advanced chemistry books before he was fourteen. In his late teens he had moved on to guns and was busy trying to design and modify them. Locals in the town used to say that you could find the family house from the mushroom-shaped cloud that was constantly hanging over it. At one point he blew up the kitchen quite comprehensively with a silver compound that turned everything black, including his face, for some days afterwards. A patch on the ceiling had to be painted over regularly for several years he adds, much to his father's annoyance.

It was some time, however, before he found an explanation for the reaction he'd accidentally encountered. His father (who was also caught in the explosion) banned all *dangerous* chemistry at that point, but the adventurous youngster still found ways to get his fix. It wasn't all accidents and catastrophes, though, as the young man also made his hobby quite an entrepreneurial one. He developed airgun pellets that exploded on impact and tiny hand-thrown bombs. Obviously, there was no shortage of kids at school willing to part with their pocket money for these devices, and he actually made quite good money selling them. So, as you can now ascertain, our intrepid boy-wonder clearly had a career mapped out for himself even from a very young age. Luckily, he chose to use those skills for good.

With such work there are always misconceptions about what's involved. How realistic is that bomb that has been depicted in countless Hollywood movies where the good guy is sweating over the decision to cut either the red or the blue wire and save the day or maybe even humanity? Colin says that Hollywood movie scenes like that are actually pretty rare in his work. Also, there are many different types of bombs and not all of them have wires. Some are so hastily assembled that the colours of the wires make absolutely no difference – it's simply a wire. The builders of these bombs are generally not intending them to be defuzed so they aren't going to make it easy for anyone to do so by colour-coding anything.

The closest he ever came to a Hollywood bomb was in Bosnia during the Yugoslav conflict. He spotted something wrong with a mine and investigated. He discovered the device functioned by using a "collapsing circuit" – in other words, cutting the wrong wire (or breaking the ultra-thin extension wire) would set it off. Luckily, it hadn't been armed so there was no sweating-brow scene with a shaky pair of pliers trying to save the day.

So what is it that he mainly deals with when he is called out on jobs all around the world? Well, there is a great deal of assessment work that doesn't necessarily mean any actual defuzing. Someone may have discovered a large stockpile of munitions from a forgotten war and needs to know what they are dealing with. Of course, a lot of his work deals with land mines that may also involve extracting them from the ground, which is no easy task. Then there are common situations like old undetonated bombs from aircraft that have lain undiscovered for long periods of time. No two jobs are ever alike, and that is the main reason why it can be such a challenging but exciting job.

Surprisingly, Colin doesn't have a great deal of fear for what he does but it isn't out of complacency. He's been doing it long enough now to be fully aware of what can go wrong but confident enough in his abilities that he knows it won't. Of the danger he's adamant that the single most dangerous aspect is the involvement of other people, who are often eager to impress. He prefers to work alone, which he does most of the time during weapon disassembly; the key is to control every aspect of the activity and environment. Other people always change the dynamics in some way, he says, and almost always for the worse.

A few years back he was working in Jordan where a senior Jordanian officer (wearing no protective equipment) was showing him and a US Colonel around a live minefield while his men were clearing mines. As he was describing operations, the man inadvertently stepped back onto a live anti-tank mine. Fortunately for Colin and the others his weight was not enough to trigger it otherwise they'd all have been killed.

He also had a very close call in Moldova, where he had instructed a supposedly, highly experienced expat operator to pack live sub-munitions in crates for demolition. The man apparently decided to throw in (literally) the detonators he'd removed and was busy driving shards of wood in amongst them to hold them in place. These are, he tells me, very delicate items and they were both incredibly lucky that nothing happened.

These are the kind of moments, he says, when you need to stand your ground and be clear to your employer that you are in charge of the operation. It is, he says, the only time he's ever refused to work with anyone, and the man was removed from the operational team immediately. Accidents can of course happen in his line of work and that's accepted, but stupidity on the other hand is not.

'I really believe that fear is mostly in the imagination and can be managed accordingly. I'd say I experience more fear and apprehension thinking about a trip to the dentist than I do dismantling an explosive device. The dentist, though, as we all know, is never as bad when you actually get there, so I use that same principle to deal with what I do in my job.'

The most dangerous incident he has ever been involved with was in Macedonia. People who work in bomb disposal over time develop their own techniques, and Colin had formulated a procedure for dismantling a cluster munition. (These types of devices are essentially bombs within bombs, whereby the main bomb detonates and sprays out other smaller bombs. They are incredibly dangerous and unpredictable and designed for mass destruction.)

What he discovered was a locally manufactured mortar bomb produced hastily during the war. The inside, he says, functioned like a giant grenade, and actually used a grenade initiator and fly-off lever, which was supposed to release the payload – the smaller bombs. Almost always, before he starts work on the procedure with someone else involved, he will demonstrate the procedure first. On this occasion it involved removing the payload very slowly to uncover the end of the fly-off lever (the trigger) so that it could be taped down to prevent it functioning. As his Macedonian friend pulled the payload out, the lever unexpectedly functioned and the ejection charge went off, impacting and burning his hands and scattering live sub munitions all over the room.

The interesting thing about cluster bombs is that the initial explosion has to be small enough so it won't detonate the smaller bombs but large enough so that it will send them far enough away to maximise the carnage, if you want to call it that. This is what saved the assistant from more serious injuries in the accident. Although Colin himself wasn't injured he says that clearing up the damaged and armed sub-munitions was one of the most dangerous jobs he's ever undertaken.

There is actually a bittersweet twist in Colin's life which I wasn't really expecting, and certainly nothing like I'd gotten from any of the other participants of this book. I get the feeling as I'm reading his answers that he's trying to tell me something because he wants someone else to hear it, but also maybe to hear himself saying it. It turns out to actually be a life lesson too valuable to just brush over.

It starts with his own father…many years ago. You might remember him from the earlier part of this chapter – the guy who banned dangerous chemistry from his house to avoid his family's demise…

Of his father, he says, more than anything, he set an incredible example of hard work, duty and selflessness. He can't recall a time when he saw him do or say the wrong thing. For a long time he assumed that everyone's father was like that, but as he grew up he realised they weren't, and not everyone was as lucky as he was. More than anything, he said, it made him realise how important it was to be a good role model and solid figure for his own kids. (Colin had two sons with his first wife, Jo – Drew and Ryan who are twenty-six and twenty-three, respectively).

There's a standing joke in the bomb disposal unit, or the formal name for it Explosive Ordnance Disposal (EOD for short), that it stands for Every One Divorced, acknowledging the pressure that working in bomb disposal puts on marriages. For some people, it may be that this line of work can just be a nine-to-five job but for the relatively few, hard-core EOD guys he says it's an all-consuming vocation. He says he's very focused and confident in his own judgement and was from time to time probably overly forceful in putting his point across in his first marriage.

'My EOD career, like others whom I worked with, tended to come first so there was potential for some partners to resent the fact that their career takes second place, which is essentially what happened to me. Often, I would have these extreme highs after finishing jobs that would bring me immense satisfaction. The difference between what these jobs were, and the realities of life, were sometimes poles apart even though I always looked forward to getting back and seeing my wife and boys. Sadly, though, the family reunions were rarely, if ever, as warm and rewarding as I'd imagine them. My wife would be tired and stressed from having to deal with everything alone and the boys would just be carrying on with everyday life – squabbling or bored, or with homework to do. Nobody would have any idea what I'd been doing, and most of the time there would be very little interest. In later years my wife never

met me at the airport and I'd just take a taxi home and let myself
in, sometimes to an empty house.'

It's always harder to see the realities of life in the moment and with hindsight you get the feeling he has definitely done a fair portion of soul-searching. He apologises for turning the story a bit negative but he wanted to be as open as possible about the realities of doing what he does and still fitting back in with normal life.

He has, however, enjoyed immensely the relationship with his boys and gets on great with them. They virtually grew up outdoors, he says, and they're both great athletes, so winning competitions featured regularly and prominently. A real highlight was Ryan being accepted for the UK Olympic rowing programme (although he's since had to quit to go to university). Drew was unable to join the forces because of a serious rugby injury, completing his training in the police.

Colin says time was always his biggest enemy and he has regrets about not spending enough time with his family or being patient enough with them for that matter. It's bittersweet, in a sense, as he's been able to do the job he loves but this ultimately cost him his relationship with his wife and he knows that. It's easy to be judgemental of him but you have to remember that he was born to do what he does and that's evident in his early attempts at blowing up the family home. It wasn't a selfish choice; he was just a young kid who followed his dreams and it took him to where he is now.

It's certainly a good lesson for anyone unable to loosen the leash of work and readdress the balance of their lives. Colin has a lot to say, and it's interesting, both in personal and workplace affairs. I wondered if he has a different view on modern-day terrorism than say, a regular person who only knows the facts from what they see on the news. News is controlled, edited to a certain extent, and I think most people realise that. Colin sees what they see first-hand and his interactions with people in those affected areas gives him a better insight into why they do what they do.

'I've always felt that many of the foot soldiers in any cause are just pawns. Energetic or angry young men are easily channelled into violence and extremism – it offers excitement and rewards that they probably couldn't get any other way. I feel a bit like that about my own military service. It just happened to be on the right/good/ acceptable side. It's the older leaders, who use them so cynically that I have a problem with, throwing them on the fire, so to speak, by using propaganda to enhance themselves and their private agenda.

You can't get the chance to talk to someone in bomb disposal without wanting to get their opinions on recent events in the world relating to terrorism. The *shoe bomber*, he says, was a fairly recent and minor influence and used probably one of the more ridiculous types of bombs ever attempted. He takes me back to 1986 and an incident which turned out to be the major factor that shaped modern-day airport security.

A Jordanian man called Nezar Hindawi attempted to blow up a Boeing 747 flying out of London. His attempt involved using his pregnant fiancée to take the devices on board without her knowledge. The genius, he explains, if you want to call it that, was that he had separated the explosive from the detonator which was cleverly hidden inside a functioning calculator. The detonator was simply set on a timer and programmed to go off when the flight was airborne. He almost got away with it had it not been for over-zealous security that potentially saved the lives of three hundred and seventy-five people and the bomber's unborn child. The Hindawi affair, as it became widely known, is the reason why we now have a separate scan of electronic devices and why we are asked...

'Did you pack your own bags?'

History is littered with bombs that failed to explode, and in 2017 such a device failed to properly go off on a tube train at Parsons Green station in London. While it did cause a few serious injuries, a lot more injuries were caused by the stampede as commuters fled the area. He says of that particular bomb that it was a lucky escape as given its size if it had gone off correctly the death toll would have been anything from twenty to thirty people.

Colin states that the Internet now has the ability to teach people how to make bombs, be it mainly rudimentary ones. He ought to know this better that anyone as his childhood activities learning how to make bombs was the exact same thing, only out of chemistry books instead. He makes a comparison between today's modern terrorist and those in the days of the IRA. It took the IRA, he says, thirty years to make the jump from simple explosive devices to sophisticated electronic ones. Now we are seeing groups like ISIS make that jump in less than a year, so the potential for their capabilities and the untold amount of deaths they could cause is almost limitless. He is exposed to all of that in his field work and sees the horror of what ordinary folk can only imagine. It's hard for him to adjust back to society after getting up close and personal with the worst kinds of human activities.

He struggled the most when witnessing people getting upset or confrontational about the little things in everyday life, having just come back from a war zone where he'd seen real problems and suffering that just didn't compare. It's a very common story of readjustment amongst soldiers and aid workers all over the world. Seeing that horror also makes him think about the boys and how he couldn't bear it if anything ever happened to them. Parents are no different in war-torn countries; they just have to deal with these horrors everyday of their lives. Having children, combined with what he does, has certainly made him feel much more vulnerable than regular folk.

He knows loss too, having lost a child, Jamie, with his first wife. Jamie was born with a heart problem and died after a very short life. It was the first time anything in his life had really gone badly wrong and it instantaneously undermined his faith in his own luck and immortality. His eyes often well with tears during quiet times when he is by himself and thinks about those final hours in the hospital. No one ever really gets over something like that, and you can't really understand the feeling unless you've been through it yourself, he tells me.

Clearly Colin's career and life certainly haven't been a bed of roses by any means. He takes it very seriously, and he needs to, when his life and the life of others are in his hands. I enquire about fatigue, wondering how on earth anyone could do what he did back then, with young babies keeping you up all hours. He says it was definitely an issue, although the boys have been sleeping well now for over twenty years so he has forgotten what the toll of that was like, he says, with possibly a wry smile. If anything, one of the greatest risks he faces is from colleagues who contribute to their own fatigue by staying out late and drinking. It's far from ideal working in his field with people whose concentration is impeded by a hangover.

The biggest issue he faces with fatigue is that clients are only willing to pay for economy class flights when he attends to their jobs. So he might jump off a plane and straight into a high-pressure situation after fighting for the armrest for twelve hours on a flight. In addition, he often faces a lot of driving situations that are statistically much more dangerous than what he does. He says any kind of activity that takes you near a road in Afghanistan means you are taking your life in your hands. The problem, he says, is that it's usually someone else behind the wheel who is more often than not trying to impress you for one reason or another. He says he hesitates to ask them to slow down but laments that they always seemed quite bewildered by the request. There have also been numerous white-knuckle rides in helicopters, sometimes while being tracked by enemies on the ground.

Continuing with the dangerous elements of the job we get onto the subject of near-death experiences. It's quite an interesting topic as the line between life and death, and what he does, is incredibly thin. If something is going to explode, and at most of its intended velocity, people, including himself, are going to die, and there is really not much else that can be said. It's a little different from some of the experiences of others in this book where they have nearly experienced death but survived all the odds – usually down to their training or condition. Suffice to say, apart from wearing an inch-thick cast-iron suit, Colin's life and death prospects are largely unknown. He says that he never really knows how close he comes to death. All devices function erratically, especially when they are old and especially when they are handmade. There is the tendency, he says, with human nature, to always push the boundaries of what you have done before many times. Confidence, while he says is an asset, can also be your own worst enemy, and he reminds himself of that on every outing.

It's a common misconception as to how dangerous his job is when you look at it in a statistical sense. You're far more likely, he says, to get killed on a building site than you are in bomb disposal. I want to say that this might be true but that there are a lot more builders than there are bomb defuzers, but I don't. He doesn't seem to fear for his life within the context of his job, so I ask him if there is anything that scares him about the world.

'I suppose, like most people, I fear zealots and fundamentalists of any persuasion. People who are so intolerant, and so sure that they're right, that they feel justified in imposing their ways on others, or are happy to pull the trigger – killing them, if they don't fit their mantra. So it mostly saddens rather than scares me, but I wonder what kind of world my children will grow up in given the radical acceleration of these kinds of divisions in society.'

He certainly tries to keep the boys close to him and encourages them to be openly affectionate with their grandparents. The boys, he says, grew up hugging their grandfather and have continued that into manhood which he enjoys. Despite having a good relationship with his own father, it was never as open as he had hoped. He tells me that about ten years ago he summoned up the courage to hug his father when they parted one day. He thinks that was difficult for his father initially but they've been doing it ever since, and that one moment has now broken a cycle he thought wasn't the best for the two of them.

Although his career isn't winding down to any degree, he does have one eye on his later years. Quite possibly, from what it sounds, he isn't particularly looking forward to retirement. He's very happy doing what he does and will continue to do so for as long as the timer allows. There will eventually be a time when he will have to leave the fieldwork and mainly concentrate on the training and office side of things. He is still very fit and exercises every day in areas such as weight training and sports like squash. It's important that he stays fit and healthy as that helps his mind in being able to concentrate for long periods of time, which is essential to, well, basically stay alive.

Unsurprisingly it has been hard at times for him to slot back into society after being where he's been and seeing what he's seen. He says there is a special bond between people that are involved in what he does. He's not trying to make it an elite club by any means, but it's certainly a hard career for those outside of it to understand.

His boys have clearly noticed what he does, since they were very young. His eldest, Drew, had clearly noticed his dad's interest in firearms and his first sentence linked to this was to a small girl in a hardware store and went…

'Get in my trolley. I've got a gun…'

I wonder how dear dad managed to defuze that one with the girl's parents. Perhaps with a *wincing* smile and a swift exit? No amount of field experience can teach you how to deal with something like that.

"The colour of the wires mean nothing"

VII
THE FREERIDE
MOUNTAIN BIKER

©Ian Collins

When the Sumerians invented the wheel around 3500 BC, little could they have imagined the kinds of uses it would have thousands of years later and in today's modern world. Given that they invented it more for an industrial or survival purpose, it would have been absolutely inconceivable for them to have imagined the kinds of sports and pursuits that it has spawned.

Freeride mountain biking is one of those modern-day sports that's taken the Sumerian's wheel and flipped it on its head. Although bikes are nothing new, they tended to be used on relatively flat surfaces. That is until someone decided that taking them *off-road* might offer more of a thrill. That said, the first versions of the modern-day mountain bike, and what was done to them compared to the incredible modern-day spectacle we see now, are about as far apart as you could imagine.

In lots of sports, abilities have evolved and changed so much in the last thirty years that it can be a little overwhelming to see something you did for fun, growing up as a kid, suddenly become this televised extreme sport that is so far removed from what you remember. It almost doesn't quite seem real or in some cases even seem physically possible. For every kid who ever rode a trail bike or a BMX bike on a dusty track back in the 1980s and caught a little bit of air off a bump or trail then this chapter is especially for you.

The definition of freeriding goes something like this: it's free in the sense that there are no limitations. There is no man-made track to race around and for the most part the riders involved find their own way down the trails that Mother Nature has created. "Trails" is probably a fairly loose way to describe the terrain on which they compete, given the obstacles they face getting from top to bottom.

Utah in the United States is one of the more famous settings on the free ride world tour as it's home to the most famous competition of all – *The Red Bull Rampage*. Utah's Mars-like landscape is covered in monolithic rock spires and prehistoric mesas, all of which make for an otherworldly-looking course that riders set about trying to tame. Essentially the competition involves choosing your own individual route down the mountain, where you are scored on the difficulty and speed of your run. The cliffs are near vertical and some of the jumps made by the riders can see them launch into the air and cover distances of up to eighty feet. That said, the riders are allowed to slightly *prep* the trails they choose, which involves a lot of digging and smoothing out of the surfaces.

It's difficult to describe the spectacle of these events. Some of the mountain faces they are trying to ascend would be out of most people's ability to get down on foot. Yet here we find them tearing down at ridiculous speeds and catching air off some enormous jumps as they go. As you can imagine though, it goes wrong every now and then. When I say wrong, I mean really wrong, and we are talking not only about career-threatening injuries, but also life-threatening ones. The athletes have to be both extremely skilled and totally fearless, and it is this that sets the best apart from the also-rans.

Cameron Zink is a "once in a lifetime athlete". There is no other way of putting it. In all sports every now and then you'll get someone come along and change the boundaries of what can be done, and for freeride mountain biking that man was Cam. Free riding is a relatively new sport and doesn't have the polished appearance of some of the more mainstream extreme sports but he, along with his fellow riders, is changing that, and very fast.

You can't really talk about Cam without talking about the performance that defined his career and changed the perception of what can be done on two wheels. At the 2013 world tour event in Utah, Cam completed the biggest backflip off the edge of a mountain ever done in a competition. It was done off a short man-made platform, some forty feet off the ground. The jump itself covered a distance of seventy-eight feet – in other words it was massively ground-breaking. From that height merely jumping off would have resulted in at least both arms and legs being broken. If you factor in the danger of the speed he was going, and the fact that he was upside down, then the possibility of serious injury or death is really quite realistic. It's little wonder that he's often compared to Evel Knievel, and I don't mention that comparison lightly. In fact, I suspect, that had the great man been there watching he would have tipped his cane to him as a sign of appreciation.

At the time of this career-making move he was expecting his first child as well, with his wife, Amanda. She's a constant on the sidelines at his event and his biggest supporter. Now aged thirty-two he's been a professional mountain biker since he was sixteen.

When Cam was very young, a friend of his dad's, Howard, brought a shiny new mountain bike into the Zink family business and Cam's dad was instantly intrigued, as at the time the concept of mountain biking was just taking its first steps. He says he doesn't think it was his dad's intention from the start to get him and his brothers riding but it turned into the best catalyst for family time and substance for them. They would travel the country going from race to race and riding with each other. His dad had very bad arthritis in his hips and could never run with the boys or play ball. It was sad in a way, Cam says, as a lot of people thought my dad was our grandpa because he had us when he was forty and was pretty slow-moving. When we got on bikes, though, we could all ride together. It was our activity and the thing to do.

Cam is unique, in a sense, because his reputation is built on his fearlessness and individuality, rather than his win or loss record. He stands out from the crowd and his fans and competitors know it. Although he's won many events through his career it's most certainly not what he will be remembered for. It became apparent, very quickly, when researching him that while he might not win every event he enters, he will invariably execute some maniacal trick that leaves everyone else mystified.

I asked him if he wished he had won more or is he happy to be that guy who steals the show from the actual winner. He says that he can't change the past and only plans for the future by just continuing to build his skill set, so it gives him the best possibility to do whatever he needs to do when an opportunity arises. Sometimes, he says, he's more focused on getting that one crazy trick done rather than winning, but that role can reverse at times. He is extremely spontaneous when it comes to an event or film trip, but is only ever truly satisfied when he feels he has done his best. Winning or losing is not so important to him. If something lines up or makes sense, he says he has to go for it because if he doesn't, then he knows he will be dissatisfied.

Cam's style of riding has certainly earned him some serious respect and turned some pretty major heads. Travis Pastrana, who is considered a god-like presence in the world of Formula motor cross, has gushed over the talented rider, something that has truly humbled him.

'It's hard to even explain. For me, someone like Travis Pastrana, even knowing who I am, blows my mind. The fact that he respects my riding and has such nice things to say about me is about the biggest compliment I could get. It's an honour to be in the position I'm in with the sport, and I am proud that my sport, which I have always pushed for, is legitimate after helping pioneer it from the beginning.'

I mention to Cam that I've spoken to a lot of elite athletes doing dangerous sports. Often they will say that they come across opponents who are more talented and fitter than they are, but the thing which gives them the winning edge in the end is their mindset about danger, and managing their fear. They just see an obstacle and they go for it without the thought or hesitation that a normal person might have before doing something dangerous. He says he thinks I've hit the nail on the head and it's a valid point that explains his attitude. Fear management is his biggest asset in his sport, and especially in his life. Fear and stress, he believes, will only cause more danger and stress.

'Do what you can and take all the resources you have to make the best decision possible and perform to the best of your ability.'

It's sometimes hard to really picture the brutality of the sport and what it can inflict on the human body. You do bear witness to the crashes that are played over and over again on the highlight reel, but after the crash comes the recovery and that's something you can never really comprehend unless you are the person involved in it. Sports' cameras tend to only want to capture the high moments or the very low moments when it all goes horribly wrong and you hear the crunching of bones on the rock-hard turf.

Cam has, I think, broken almost as many bones and snapped as many ligaments and tendons as Evel Knievel, and Evel took some pretty big hits and still came out fighting. Cam's list of injuries is long – very, very long. There was the broken foot, tibia, and hand (three times). Then the three anterior cruciate ligament ruptures, one of which is enough to end a career. Then add to that a dislocated wrist and a couple of displaced shoulders and you have a list that is almost too painful to comprehend. Thankfully he did not have to have his spleen removed after rupturing it twice. I start to wonder what would happen to the guy if he ever damaged his heart, but it seems to be made of cast iron.

Although Cam is very high profile in his world he is sometimes a man of few words and lets his actions speak louder than his words. The injuries have been hard, he says, but at the end of the day he wanted to push the boundaries as far as he could, while making sure that he got more out of mountain biking than it got out of him. That's probably the best way you can sum up his internal drive to push the envelope.

Speaking of stress and the ability to control it, you have to spare a thought for Cam's parents, Lenna and Howard, who have had to deal with their fair share of worry over the years from Cam's aerial antics. I was lucky enough to be able to converse with both of them and I wanted to continue down the path that tries to explain the reason for his success. Was it something he was born with, or that developed with age?

Of her son, his mother Lenna says that right from birth he was hollering and fighting. The staff at the hospital actually failed to get an accurate reading when he was first weighed such was the frenzy of the young boy's movements. He was an easy birth but there were a lot of complications during the pregnancy. Her firstborn, Howie, was the exact opposite in that it was a fairly easy pregnancy but one hell of a birth. She wonders if it was the trauma Cameron suffered over those nine months which played a part in developing his tenacity and fighting spirit that's made him the fearless superstar that he is today. The brothers are also very close and there is a degree of admiration and idolisation between them that plays out very nicely in their lives.

I can't quite let Lenna go without questioning her about Cam's supposedly high IQ. Rumours continue to circulate about his supposed genius status and I'm curious to find out. It is discussed in his documentary *Reach for the Sky* but never divulged and I'm eager to discover what the real number is. With some prompting she does eventually give it up but with the agreement that I don't publish it. What I can say though, is that it's high, and at a level that puts Cameron in a very unique position as both a super athlete and someone who could easily understand the Projectile Motion Formula of his death-defying jumps. Sure, Einstein was smart, but he couldn't do a backflip off his desk let alone off a hundred-foot mountain.

Cam's dad has a slightly less complicated story about his youngest son's early signs of fight and determination. Howard recalls the time the family relocated from Lake Tahoe to Carson City, which are neighbouring states in the north-west of the United States. It was the usual tough adjustment, Howard says, of the boys fitting in to their new neighbourhood and coming to grips with the pecking order. He recounts the day that elder brother, Howie, was being picked on by one of the older boys on the block. Younger brother, Cam who was only four and a half years old, decided he had seen enough and stepped in to mediate. It's worth noting that Howie was not a small kid, certainly no slouch, and more than capable of holding his own. Cam, however, wasn't willing to take any chances on his brother's behalf and marched straight up and whacked the offender in the back with a plastic baseball bat that was lying on the lawn. Cam, as his dad says, made quite a name for himself that day, and this was the start of the legendary status that he now enjoys as an adult.

Cam's kindergarten teacher also noticed an inkling of the adventurous side and took his mother aside one day to have a quiet word…

'I have a son just like Cameron. Remember, it's not a matter of preventing him from jumping off the cliff, but rather, guiding him to the cliff which will hurt him the least, because he will jump!'

That proverbial cliff his teacher spoke about is never far away with the man though, and visits to it have only become more frequent later in life. While Cam's aforementioned injury list is very long and painful it comes as a bit of a surprise that in fact he's only had one injury that could have taken his life.

One day he was riding a very simple trail when he fell. It wasn't a bad fall, but unbeknown to him he had fallen in such a way that a twig on the ground had stabbed him in the groin so hard that it had actually burst the main artery to his leg. The problem was that the twig had not broken the skin and only caused internal damage.

'I was losing a lot of blood internally but as it had nowhere to go it built up a lot of pressure inside my leg. Luckily, though, by a freak occurrence the swelling and the pressure it created happened in such a way that it stopped the artery bleeding. The doctors told me later in hospital that had that twig penetrated the skin I would have bled to death without question, no two ways about it. It's a bit scary to look back now and realise that.'

Others in his sport have not been so lucky. There have been many casualties in the last few years, he says, and that has been rough. Kelly McGarry died of heart complications while riding. Two other friends, Erik Roner and Stevie Smith, both died doing other extreme sports not related to their mountain bike activities. Dave Mirra, a legend in the sport of BMX, sadly recently committed suicide. Although Cameron did not know him he understands that he was suffering from mental health issues due to the multiple head traumas he had suffered over the course of his career.

A friend of Cam, with whom he had been riding since the age of thirteen, Paul Basagoitia, was paralysed at the *Red Bull* Rampage a few years back. Happily though, Paul is actually now riding a little and walking a few steps without canes or crutches. Cameron says the progress he has made is inspiring, but also says it's still the biggest fear for him, maybe even over death.

Cam says the sport, in his opinion, isn't really an endurance one, or really even that physical, until you hit the ground in a crash. If everything went to plan and every time you rode it was perfect, you could be fairly unhealthy and weak. It's the small corrections when things go wrong or the major failures when you hit the ground for which you really need conditioning, which is why he tries to keep as fit as possible. He actually tries to not "train". He finds that regimented training just doesn't suit his personality. He says he did recently hire a trainer, but usually he's in and out of town so much, or dealing with smaller injuries where he was unable to train, that the guy was getting mad at him. He loves to stay active and will try to ride as many different disciplines and styles of mountain biking, as well as motocross, snowboarding, surfing.

'The mind is the most powerful muscle, and staying sane is tough in our sport. Many have come, risen to the top, and quit during my career. My attribute to longevity is staying happy and keeping it fun. The best way to prepare for everything that a riding career will throw at you is practise and experience and that only comes from how much time you spend on the seat.'

That time on the seat does come with its downsides though, as Cam has to spend time away from his family to fulfil his obligations to his career. It's better now than it used to be when he first started out, but he is still away from the family for an average of four months a year. He is married to Amanda, whom he describes as the woman of his dreams. They also have two children together: a girl called Ayla who is five and a boy called Asher who is one year old. The eldest is already a mad keen bike rider and will throw her hand at any sport from surfing to snowboarding. One suspects she has inherited a bit of her dad's daredevil streak which might give her mum and grandma something to worry about in a few years' time. Although I'm not sure it's going to worry her dad much, and you get the feeling like his father before him, he'll be there cheering her on from the sidelines. Cam says he always wanted a family but would probably have put it off till he was forty just like his own father. Alya had other ideas!

Once you've watched a few of Cam's YouTube clips and movies you start to realise that you get to see his wife cry a lot. She can be seen at many competitions with her face buried in her hands sobbing as she is unable to deal with the worry of watching her husband risk his life backflipping off mountains. You see, she is privy to exactly what tricks he is going to try and knows the dangers. It's slow torture for her as the moment arrives, but her elation when he makes it through alive is also quite heart-warming. She's spent enough nights in hospital with him and his broken body to know how close he teeters on the edge of what is humanly possible on a mountain bike. He says she definitely has the hardest job on the mountain being married to what others say is a complete nutcase. He has made her cry numerous times on national and international television, but luckily, usually in fear and then happiness and relief.

When I ask if he and Amanda ever talk about the dangers of his job now that they are parents, he replies that they have an understanding that he will devote as much time as possible to the family while trying to keep himself as safe as possible on the trail. Inevitably, he says, one day he won't ride. But for now he will be pushing it for as long as possible. Afterwards, he insists, there will be a long life of safety, although I'm not sure how much he really means by that last promise.

In the early days of his career it was really hard to make a living from the sport. As it was a new and upcoming sport the corporate world that manufactures its equipment wasn't quite ready to take on the fully paid sponsorship role. During this period he was tossed around like a rag doll from sponsor to sponsor on a path littered with broken promises. Ultimately, he ended up funding most of his own travel which was hard as much of it involved travelling to other countries to compete.

That hunger to be able to compete led him down the path to starting his own business. In 2009 he started a company called *Sensus,* which manufactures handgrips for his bikes. Anyone who has ever started a small business knows that it can be tough, but especially so if you're a professional athlete with massive restraints on your time. He admits that for quite some time he was actually packing and posting the products himself along with his wife. Not many customers, I'd imagine, would expect that their handlebar grips had the actual fingerprints of the rider himself on them.

With *Sensus* an economic success and valuable business experience gained, Cam convinced his major bike sponsor to let him run the division of their company when they expanded into North America. On top of that he runs two businesses as well as a non-profit company called *Sensus* R.A.D which is dedicated to getting bike trails built and funded. The man certainly knows how to get things done and has built an amazing life for himself and his family using both his physical and mental talents. That's not to say that every now and then he slips up, like the time he left the house when he was looking after his daughter who was napping, having completely forgotten that she was in the house.

'I still see the look on my wife's face that day as it's burned into my memory. Although I do not wish to see it in person for as long as I live.'

Cam can also lay claim to being in the pages of *The Guinness Book of Records* for the biggest ever backflip done on a bike. A one-hundred-foot monster of a jump that really needs to be seen to be believed. It takes imagination and a whole lot of guts to be a leader in this type of sport but Cam has it in buckets.

The adrenaline highs that athletes like Cam experience are some of the greatest that one can feel as a human. The adrenaline comes not only from their stunts but also from the adulation they receive from the fans who come to watch them. He says that the feeling landing that backflip in Utah was something he will never forget. He mentions that he is sure that when the time comes to hang up his pedals he's going to miss that elation he feels through extreme riding. However, he wants to go out on his own terms and be satisfied he got the best out of himself every time he rode, regardless of whether he wins or loses.

"Backflips off mountains"

VIII
THE SURF PHOTOGRAPHER

C hances are if you picked up a surfing magazine in the last forty years you wouldn't be able to flick through the pages too far before you came across a picture taken by Brian Bielmann. He is, to say the least, somewhat of a legend. He's seen the sport evolve through his lenses and has overseen the rise of many a champion over his stellar career. His photography has become somewhat iconic and he is much loved by the surfing community the world over who gawp at his seemingly amazing ability to produce the world's most mouth-watering surf photography.

It's probably necessary at this point to explain a little bit about what's involved in his work. The immediate reaction I would assume from most people, when they see the word, photographer, in a book about daredevils, is to wonder exactly how it qualifies to be there in the first place. It's easy to see the logic of including a big wave surfer or a lifeguard but perhaps not so obvious to associate a surfing photographer with a life-threatening or perilous activity. Rest assured that his place is well and truly earned here, as to shoot big waves from the water, as he does all winter in Hawaii, is right up there as being just as dangerous as the surfing itself.

If you've ever watched professional surfers take on large waves of consequence at breaks like the famous *Pipeline* in Hawaii then you will have undoubtedly spotted a few hapless souls, cameras in hand, bobbing up and down in the water trying to capture the action. The art of being a great photographer in the ocean is to get as close as possible to the surfer riding the wave, which means being able to position yourself at the very crest of the wave as the surfer passes by underneath. At many places in Hawaii the waves are famous for barrelling which means that the wave breaks in such a way that the rider is actually able to travel inside the curl of it as it thunders across the reef.

Getting a good shot of a surfer inside the wave is the bread and butter of the surf photographer, that's for sure. Getting so close to the breaking lip is dicing with death though, as if one gets too close to the breaking wave one can be sucked over the falls and pounded on the shallow reef. Getting sucked over the falls basically means that you become part of the wave as it breaks and it's the cause of most of the serious injuries for both surfer and photographer alike. Quite often to get the perfect shot means one needs to wait until the very last moment as the lip hurls over the rider. You'll often see pictures of surfers inside the barrel and then a random arm or two sticking out just a few metres away holding a camera. When you get as good at water photography as people like Brian you're able to take the perfect shot virtually blind. It's also no surprise at all to find out that many surfing photographers have lost their lives on the job. However, just like the surfers whom they are trying to capture, it's accepted as part and parcel of the job.

Brian is down-to-earth. He loves a beer but also warms a pew every Sunday at his local church. During the early eighties the house he shared with first wife, Gina, was somewhat of a focal point for parties on the north shore of Oahu in Hawaii and was certainly the place to be seen. Though the crazy days of the eighties are long gone he still is as social as ever and always up for a laugh with friends.

Oahu is a tight-knit community of which he has been a part ever since he transplanted himself from chilly Virginia in mainland USA to the tropical shores of Hawaii back in 1975. He seems genuinely enthusiastic to be included in the book. Surfing photographers tend to be a thankless lot and I get the feeling he's quite pleased to be recognised for doing what he has done for the last forty years.

I figured I'd test his sense of humour straight up, when I mention his first wife, Gina. She was, in the mid to late eighties, the quintessential blonde swimwear model, and she had a very successful career adorning the pages of many a surfing magazine. Brian actually shot a lot of her photos. I figured before we started that I'd better tell him that as a teenager a number of friends and I had posters of her up on our bedroom walls and had a fairly large crush on her. With this fact he is highly amused and informs me that he gets that a lot from guys in their forties that he meets. He most certainly sees the funny side of things.

I asked him whether started surfing because he was a surf photographer or the other way around? It turns out that he simply needed to make a living when he was twenty-one and photography seemed like the perfect job where he'd be able to keep surfing but work on the beach as well. The surfing industry back then wasn't the billion-dollar business that it is now so it was definitely a bit of a gamble. He bought all the equipment but for several months it just lay there gathering dust. Just then he suffered a near fatal accident whilst surfing where he hit the reef head first in a bad wipe-out. The injury got badly infected and he was actually quite lucky to have survived it.

'The hole in my head was so big that doctors ordered me to stay out of the water for thirty days. I guess that's when I decided to start using that camera equipment, and the rest is history. Although I do wonder sometimes what would have happened had I not had that life-threatening injury. I've been lucky though, as it's afforded me a blessed life and the people I've met and places I've seen have created a wonderful back catalogue of memories.'

The memories of his own work live large in the surfing population as well. Most good-to-average photographers might shoot valiantly their entire career and never get a shot good enough to make the front cover of a surfing magazine. Brian typically delivers covers like shelling peas and has so far amassed almost two hundred shots that were deemed good enough to sell a publication. It's an extraordinary figure when you really think about it, being, on average, five cover shots a year, considering there really aren't that many surfing publications worldwide and that they typically only come out once a month. So, as you can see, to get that many shots of that calibre year after year means that Brian, bar maybe one or two other notable snappers, is simply in a league of his own.

He also has to be pretty versatile to be a successful surf photographer. Different waves and different situations call for changing one's game plan constantly. It's about preparing the day before, he says. Getting all your equipment together; making sure everything is in working order; and a lot of phone calls to other surfers or photographers as to what to expect.

When he knows it's going to be big then there is a fair portion of psyching yourself up as well, he tells me. These ocean-going photographers never truly know what will present itself the next day so they often need to make very quick, spontaneous decisions. Deciding if it's better to shoot from the water or the beach is usually the first decision.

If Brian has to shoot from the water then it does get trickier as often he is on his own with a camera and a pair of flippers. This is where surf photography can get really dangerous as you're sitting lower in the water than say a surfer might be sitting on a board, so there is less chance you'll see large waves approaching. There is also a fair chance you might be struck by a board as well which happens more often than you might think. Brian does on occasion employ the use of a jet ski which can get him in and out of the water a lot easier but it certainly does not mean that nothing can go wrong.

He was shooting about twenty years ago at an event at the famous Pipeline break and getting rides in and out on the jet skis. On his third time out the driver of his jet ski started acting erratically. As they were going back and forth, waiting for a chance to blast through the huge walls of white water the driver kept turning really sharply, eventually throwing Brian off the back of the ski. He was able to hold on to the seat but wasn't feeling as confident in his abilities as he should be. The driver finally saw what he considered a break where the waves were small enough to get through and headed into it full charge. Brian was clinging on the back of the ski on a big boogie board connected to the back of the ski, one hand holding the board and the other holding his camera in front of him.

'I remember seeing this wave and thinking "I think this wave is too big and maybe I should let go", but decided that the driver knew what he was doing so I decided I would just hang on. We hit the wave full force. The jet ski went vertical, the driver jumped off and the ski landed on top of me and sandwiched me between the ski and the boogie board. Somehow the water kept the thing from

squashing me but I was holding the camera in front of me and the darn thing hit me right in the eye! I was very dazed and suddenly felt something knock me over. It was the jet ski rolling over me again as yet another wave pushed it into me.'

Unfortunately for Brian he was quite badly wounded just above his eye. The camera had hit him so hard that it had cracked the ¾ inch plexiglass housing that surrounds it. While he managed to come out of the affair with just a very black eye, he was remarkably lucky not to be blinded or be knocked unconscious and drown.

Brian became a father a little later in life than most, at the age of thirty-six, with his first wife, Gina, with whom he had a son called Jesse, who is now twenty-five. He then went on to have two more children with his second wife, Shawna – Tea Renee and Tai who are nineteen and eighteen respectively. His sons are handsome and robust as you might expect, and the girl as pretty as a picture. I asked Brian if he had any regrets about having to be away a lot for work when they were young, travelling around the world shooting pictures.

'I had to spend a lot of time away from my family for sure, constantly working to pay off bills and credit cards. Then you look back and feel as though you did not spend enough time with the kids. I guess I must have done something right though, as we all get on really well. It was always really important for me to let them know they were loved. I grew up with a father who I really never lived with, as my parents divorced when I was young, and then a step father who was never very affectionate towards us. He never said he loved us and we were never able to talk about our feelings. We are now closer as we have gotten older, but the opportunity for us to bond when I was young has now passed. I've made plenty of mistakes as a dad but I tell them I love them all the time and that's the most important thing.'

I asked Brian if he thinks his own kids ever worried about what he did, and he said that his youngest child definitely had some worries. For a while Tai got really freaked out, Brian said, although he's gotten better now. There were times when he'd ask his dad if he was going in the water, especially when he got older. He's also not immune to fear either. He recalls one Christmas Day when he decided not to shoot from the water. He says it was the perfect day and the conditions were outstanding but the waves were gigantic. However, he thought to himself that if he died that day then his kids would never be able to enjoy Christmas again as it would be the anniversary of his death.

You can't really question someone who bobs up and down in the water all day without broaching the subject of shark attacks. While Brian says he tries not to think about it, he and his peers are really quite defenceless against the ocean's deadliest predators. While he tries not to think about it he has had a few close calls. He once arranged to meet up with a friend to surf and shoot photos on a particular day and at a particular time. He ended up getting delayed and changed his plans. He found out later that there was a shark attack where a surfer lost his leg at the spot he would have been at and at the exact time he would have been there if his plans had not been cancelled.

His closest call though, came in Tahiti a few years back. He had been shooting all day from the water and when he came back to the boat a friend told him there had been an eight-foot shark swimming near him, watching him the whole time. Apparently he wasn't that worried about telling him as there were so many fish around that the shark didn't seem hungry! Later that day as they left for the air strip in the car he waved goodbye to an old Tahitian man he had met previously who was on the edge of the beach cleaning the fish he had caught that day.

When they got to the air strip and were waiting for their flight the old man suddenly showed up with a trash bag taped to him and covered head to toe in blood. It was understood that the same shark who had been watching him went crazy because of the blood from the fish the old man was cleaning. It actually came out of the water and bit his leg while he was sitting on the edge of the shore. He ended up taking the same flight and there was an ambulance waiting to get him to the hospital. Brian tells me he thinks he was very lucky that day.

The talk of sharks tempts me to ask about a famous neighbour of his, Bethany Hamilton, who was the young girl who tragically lost an arm in a shark attack many years back. She recently became a mother herself and is fast becoming a big wave legend herself despite what should have been a career-ending injury. Brian says,

'Bethany Hamilton is one of the most amazing surfers and human beings in the world. She is so determined to live her life to the fullest and not allow her disability to be even considered in what she does. That means on occasion beating the world's best female surfers with literally one hand tied behind her back. Amazingly, she surfs better now than she ever did when she had both her arms. To see her do the things she does right in front of your eyes is a humbling moment. There is a reason she is one of the most famous people in the world. She seems to have no fear, ultimate faith in God, and feels she has actually been blessed because of how many people she has inspired and how many lives she has touched.'

As we change subjects, I ask Brian what effect the change from traditional film to digital had on his work. After all, he has succeeded in both eras and remembers what it used to be like when cameras were not waterproof and had to be housed in waterproofed plexiglass boxes. Anyone who started shooting in the last fifteen years will never know the toil or the hardships of waterproof boxes. It's amazing, really, given what was involved, that any decent photos ever got taken pre-digital. From the housings leaking and destroying the film, to the boxes steaming up and the focus not being quite right. He says that back then they used to swim out with thirty-six photos on one roll of film and had to choose all their exposures and actually focus. Now, with digital, you get two thousand photos and everything is automatic, so everything is a lot easier. Unfortunately for Brian that means a hundred more photographers and a billion great images, and it's now harder than ever to make a living.

He talks about his generation looking down on self-promoters as if they were a different breed. They had time, he says, to experience things, take it all in. It was not instantaneous gratification like it is now with digital images flying around the Internet minutes after they have been taken. When you got a picture published you got to see it in a magazine for a whole month and that image was burned in your mind, and that of every other surfer. Now, he says, it's all about your *fifteen minutes of fame*. Modern-day surf photographers, he says, are all fighting over Instagram and they are the best self-promoters the industry has ever seen. While he tries to keep up with them he doesn't think he was made for these times, with just a hint of nostalgia in his voice.

He jokes about the subject when we get to the issue of life insurance for what he does and that he has always paid fairly low premiums. They simply don't regard what he does as dangerous enough to justify a large yearly rate to cover the possibly of death or injury. He says it's been the least painful cheque he writes out every year for decades. Hopefully, the wool will remain permanently pulled over the watchful eyes of insurance companies until he finally hangs up his boots. It's comical really when you consider the events that unfolded for Brian during a major big wave contest a few years back.

The Eddie Aikau contest in February 2016, at the famous Waimea Bay in Hawaii, was held in the biggest waves ever contested. He's lived there a long time and had never seen anything quite like it. There were waves of up to sixty feet (twenty metres) breaking over the reef. Usually there is a large patch of very deep water next to where the wave breaks meaning that it creates a safe channel where it's too deep for the wave to break. However, on this day the waves were so big there wasn't a channel and they were breaking the whole width of the bay. The photographers were constantly having to race over the waves on the jet skis to keep from getting caught while trying to shoot the surfers.

Midway through the event a huge wave began to break in front of them and they started racing as fast as they could to get over it. The ski driver decided at the last minute that they weren't going to make it and had to do a very fast U-turn and turn towards shore and try to outrun this huge wave with a forty-foot wall of white water bearing down on them. At one point the driver leaned back to Brian and said, 'You may have to jump.' He didn't know if we could outrun it. Luckily, they made it all the way to the shore and Brian was able to hold on. He said…

'When we finally made it back out to the line-up we were screaming and hooting because we survived. It was the scariest moment of my life and I still can't believe we both made it out alive.'

In terms of fame Brian can actually claim to have shot the best surfing photo of all time: a towering avalanche of a beast that broke on a famous day in Tahiti at a spot called Teahupoo. It was ridden by legendary big wave charger, Nathan Fletcher. Brian is typically humble about the photo and tries to brush it off as maybe in the top five. Few photos, however, come even close to it in terms of the timeless moment it captured. It's also widely regarded as the heaviest wave ever ridden, and won the rider, Nathan, many accolades.

The day the photo was shot the coastguards were not letting any boats go out as the waves were so dangerous. Boats, he says, were having to sneak out through the harbour, and he managed to get himself on one. He had been out at that spot in Tahiti for almost every big swell but when he saw the first set of waves he was terrified. There were fifty boats full of photographers all trying to get into the small area from where you can view the wave the best. Later, he came to realise, that his boat was always the last one to make it over the wave. If they had been taken by a wave there was a fairly good chance they wouldn't have made it back to shore alive.

However, the precarious position of the boat is the reason why he got the best shot. All the other boats were shooting the wave from on top looking down into it. Brian's boat was still at the bottom and could still see all the white water. This is what gave the shot its *David and Goliath* look. That wave, he says, should never have been ridden, It's the craziest wave ever ridden by a human being – hands down. He tells me when he got back to the house and stuck the card in the reader and waited to see it on the screen that he got on his knees and prayed to God and said… *'I'm asking for this one to be sharp and in focus. I don't care about any of the other ones.'* When it popped up perfect on the screen he knew he had struck gold and it really probably is the best surf photo ever shot.

Brian is slowly starting to look back over his shoulder and realise just what an amazing career and life he's had. He's planning a book to celebrate forty years as a surfing photographer, and what a book it will be. Although he's sixty-one, there is still plenty of life left in the man yet, and he's got plenty to keep him busy too. His kids, his endless music collection, and his photography all fill his days.

He says he's already tried wedding photography once, but the pressure of it all just got too much. He would rather take a beating at twenty-foot *Pipeline* than deal with an unsatisfied bride and groom, and an out-of-focus wedding photo. Well, I suppose every daredevil has his own personal kryptonite.

"Shooting within the chaos"

IX
THE HUMAN CANNONBALL

It's probably one of the most familiar situations any family can face: when the main breadwinner is struck down with illness or injury, the whole family has to pull together to help each other through the tough times, and for David Smith it was no different. When David's father sustained a serious back injury at work he immediately left his summer job painting beach houses in North Carolina and went back home to help out his dad in the family business. However, this was no ordinary family business as his dad, David Snr, was at the time the world's premier human cannonball. David was drafted in by his dad as a replacement while they were halfway through the year's tour. As they say in show business "the show must go on".

Now, don't worry, David knew what was in store for him on his arrival and he had even been shot out of a cannon a few times when he was seventeen in the family's front yard in Oregon. Most families have BBQs as a way of socialising and staying close but if you grew up in the Smith family you just stood around and waited your turn to be shot through the air. It was a big step at the age of nineteen to be thrust into the limelight and face stadiums of cheering fans. Turns out though, that the job fitted him perfectly. He said that almost immediately after his first show he knew this career fitted his personality and that he would be able to take the whole thing pretty much as far as it could go.

It's been twenty years since his first show when he replaced his dad. In that time he has performed more than six thousand firings from a cannon. Once, very notably, he was given a countdown from the man who made a career out of firing people – Donald Trump. He laughs about this and you get the feeling it's certainly been a wild ride along the way. As far as careers go, it's definitely one of the more extreme ones, but it's what he loves and he's raised all his four children around it.

Now, thirty-nine years old, he resides in Florida where he spends his free time with his kids, and the rest of the time travelling from state to state or country to country, thrilling audiences with his daredevil antics. To the audience, the obvious danger before the shoot is very plain to see. The cannon is large, the distance is great and the net really isn't that big.

As a true showman, David 'The Bullet' Smith loves to play up to the crowd before the action and can be witnessed almost dancing along the cannon barrel bringing the crowd to a rapturous applause. Then as he stands aloft, the cannon starts to slowly rise and he makes his way to the end of the barrel. As it rises steeper still he lowers one leg into the barrel to stop himself sliding off and rides it all the way to its calculated angle. Bearing in mind he is now twenty-five feet from the ground, it's dangerous enough to be a show in itself. He'd probably survive a fall at this point but it would be high enough to break a few bones. Then he waves his final good bye before descending into the open barrel only to reappear like magic a short time later sailing through the sky at a formidable pace. He effortlessly glides at distances of up to nearly sixty metres before slowly somersaulting mid-air and landing neatly (he hopes) in the net on his back. There are very few spectacles like it and even though it lasts for only a few seconds you can imagine that most of the young children, and a fair portion of the adults, who watch his show probably dream what it would be like to be in his shoes.

What does go through a man's head as he's being torpedoed through the air? Surprisingly, quite a lot, as David explains, and it's not really a time to relax and enjoy the ride as in those few seconds many things can happen and many small adjustments need to be made.

'Usually when I exit the cannon the first thing I think is – I have survived. Then it's either the realisation that the exit was a good firing or it totally sucked. If it's a good one I do give myself a brief moment to enjoy the ride. If it's a bad one then I'm thinking I have to fix this one really quickly as there are things I can do mid-air to alter the outcome. Whatever happens, good or bad, it comes time to somersault mid-air which I need to do so I can land nicely on my back on the safety net. I can usually tell by this point if the landing is going to be good or bad but occasionally it's really hard to take your eyes off the net as you have that moment of blindness where you can't see the landing. The landing itself, if done perfectly, can feel as light as landing on a bed of feathers or

if it goes badly it feels like being hit by a train. The differences are just that drastic.'

The maths and calculations that are actually involved in a cannon shot are a lot more complicated than you might think. At the speed and velocity that David is shot through the air he is as susceptible to many variables from Mother Nature. Wind is obviously a big factor as well as humidity. Anything that alters the space he travels through can have a huge impact on how far he travels, or doesn't travel, depending on how you look at it. The spectacle of what David does is about as intense as it gets. Every shot he does is like the last gasp three-point shot in the NBA finals and he is the Michael Jordan of the moment every single time.

It's such a short, fleeting event that most people wouldn't stop to think about the incredible preparations that go into every shot. When we are talking about preparations though, we are talking first and foremost about the mental aspect of what David does. David alluded earlier in our conversation to how right from the start he realised that the role he had taken on from his father on short notice was one that suited him well. Once you truly fathom that he exits that cannon hundreds of times a year, only then can you start to understand that the risk factor and the possibility of death at every shot. He's been shot out of a cannon thousands and thousands of times and although it has gone wrong plenty of times, and he's nearly missed the net, he's always thankfully survived. The perimeter rope isn't as forgiving as the net itself so he could really injure himself if he landed on that.

'On one of those really bad shots I was sometimes a few inches from death. If I had missed the net I would have died. There is just no other possibility and it's as simple as that. I've mangled my knees and various other body parts on a few occasions and my kids have seen me hit the net in such a way that I was unable to do much more than grovel on the ground in pain.'

So what constitutes a near-death experience when you are the world's premiere human cannonball? He's on his second cup of coffee for the morning and is starting to get a little animated which is exactly the right frame of mind to be in to tell his stories. He was in Canada doing a show for the National Exhibition a few years back. It was kind of a big deal, he says, and expectations were very high, which can happen when you do two firings in a day. People from the first show tend to stick around to see the second, and the buzz kind of hits the folks who arrive later.

It was, he says, the most beautiful crisp blue sky of days and ideal for doing what he does best. The first shot of the day went perfectly. As time approached for the second firing everything seemed to be going well and all the safety checks had been put in place. Mother Nature though, it seems, had other plans that day and just as David climbed on top of the cannon for the pre-show build-up he suddenly felt a cool change sweep across the stadium. To his horror, looking around, every flag that had been limp ten seconds ago was suddenly flying solidly sideways. There is, of course, a degree of wind he can fly through that won't affect his trajectory but this was getting right up there close to that limit. He then gave his crew that look that said… *Let's get on with this before things get any worse.*

He says that on that particular day he had a deep sinking feeling in the pit of his stomach that something might go wrong, and that made it extremely hard to concentrate.

'I remember how much the wind had strengthened the instant I exited the cannon. The first big gust instantly threw me off course to the left and I knew straight away that I was in trouble.'

People who watch his events might not think it's really possible to think in that brief moment you're in the air but when you're as deeply focused as David is, it's certainly possible to do so. Time, he says, seems to slow down when you're in the air, and his only focus is getting himself to the net safely. In the end the wind had blown him so far of course that he landed on his backside on the edge of the net which is very unforgiving. Although he was thrown towards the middle of the net when he landed, unfortunately his body was contorted in such a way that his knee was badly tweaked out in the process. It did, he says, swell up to the size of a football and went all sorts of pretty purple colours. Despite that disaster he actually thinks of himself as being very lucky. Had the wind thrown him off even a quarter of a degree more, then he'd have missed the net altogether.

'Every shoot I do even after the thousands I've done is always a learning experience and I've taken plenty away from that one, believe you me.'

It's pretty interesting to listen to David talk about the mindset that he needs to have in the build-up to every shoot. He describes it as being "perfectly on point". While he doesn't proclaim to be a Zen master or meditation expert he does have the ability to be able to deal with the seriousness of what he does and tune out all the white noise around him. Essentially, as he says, he can think when he's scared, something that most people cannot do at all to any degree. People do some fairly unpredictable things when cornered by fear but none of this has a place in any part of what makes up the mindset of the world's premier human cannonball.

I asked David if there was ever a point when he thought he had become addicted to either the adrenaline rush of what he does or the attention that it brings him. He's pretty honest about the adrenaline part and says that in the early days he definitely succumbed to the powers of one of the body's most powerful chemicals. If you wanted to give your average human the biggest hit of a chemical the likes of which they had never felt before then surely being shot out of a cannon at mach five might be a good way to start – possibly closely followed by BASE jumping or parachuting.

He realised fairly quickly that if he was going to continue what he was doing with a young family, and keep himself safe and make the right decisions, then he really needed to try and wean himself off that kick that every shoot gave him and try to focus purely on the job at hand. He says the decision that he took gradually led him to another addiction and a much, much healthier one. He happily admits that he now thrives on the mindset of being perfectly on point or in layman's terms, being so in tune with the cannon, and the job of getting himself from the cannon to the net, that he really doesn't need any more of a high, especially when he has four young kids relying on him. I suspect that the adrenaline rush is still there for him but it sits more in the background.

When you've experienced that same thrilling moment over and over again it gets easier to control your reactions to it. David gets plenty of practice and at his peak a few years back he was doing as many as 450 cannonballs a year. The logistics alone of the whole set-up are astonishing enough considering he has to do much of it by himself, with the help of a very small crew. Over the years he has been shot over and through just about everything you could imagine, from ferris wheels to burning rings of fire, and survived all of it.

He also holds the world record for the longest distance achieved by a human being shot out of a cannon. This world record event took place in Milan, Italy, in March 2010 for a television show. He reached a total distance of 193 feet, 8.8 inches (59.05 m). The distance was measured from the mouth of the cannon to the farthest point reached on the net. David was launched by a 26'3" (8 m) long cannon. It was estimated that he travelled at a speed of 74.6 mph (120 km/h) reaching a maximum altitude of 75'6" (23 m). It's a very, very long way and extremely nail-biting to watch. You have to remember that there have been a few deaths over the years from this type of activity and it's something that David is also aware of. After all, he's not only been doing it for some time but he had also been watching his father do it before that as well. Ironically, it was actually his father's record that he broke.

Family life is a big part of this man's life, and he is very proud to have shared this with his children along the way. I asked him if he thinks they worry at all about what he does. He says that they are all smart enough to know when he is nervous but at the same time they know that he's very capable as well. He mentions, jokingly, that from when they were young they sort of grew up thinking that he was some sort of superman type character. I mean, who wouldn't? When you've followed your father around the country watching him fly through the air from a young age it would be hard not to.

David has always involved his children in what he does and they have all travelled to every state in the USA with him, as well as up to fifteen different countries for his international shows. In the early days his daughter, Alexa, from his first marriage to Stacy, now eighteen, actually grew up on the road with him as he had custody of her from about the age of two until she was eight. She was home-schooled during that time and they have a very close bond as he does with all his children. He later remarried his partner Audrey and went on to have three more children…Chloe who is thirteen, and twins Maverick and Mackenzie who are eleven. Although now separated after seven years of marriage they still co-parent amicably together. The logistics of taking children on the road wasn't always easy but it was of paramount importance in order to keep the family together when they were young. Given that David's job isn't dissimilar to the movements of a travelling salesman, hopping from state to state, it was either take the kids wherever possible or miss out on a fair portion of them growing up. He is able to travel with them during the summer and then visits them during the school year. Although it might seem like a weird and wonderful life to those on the outside, to David and his kids it's just as normal to them as normal is to anyone else.

When you spend a good portion of your life on the road going from event to event, and sometimes with your family, it's essential that you're super organised. The rig that he needed to get equipment from show to show when they did travel with him is not too far away from a semi-trailer. It has to carry the cannon itself, which is thirty feet long, as well as a host of other equipment like sound systems and the vast net set-up that he will eventually land in after the shot.

He arrives early in the morning, sometimes after having driven through the night, only to be faced with a set-up in a strange location that he's never seen before. Then he and his small crew have to set up the entire show ready for the day's performance. Again, this is where the mathematics of how the shot is set up really comes into play. It does sound a bit old school in this day and age of computers but David has compiled the most detailed logbook of every shot he's ever done. He is then able to look back over that log before every shot and decide where the net is placed in relation to the cannon. As mentioned earlier it's a fairly critical equation when it comes to finding X, as he puts it. X is where he lands in the middle of the net if it goes perfectly. If he lands either side, say, he will probably survive but not if he strays too far off the trajectory path.

I enquire about life insurance. He laments with a very dry wit that over the years there have certainly been the odd conversation or two with insurance folk about just how dangerous his job is and what kind of premiums he should be paying. You almost wish you could have been a fly on the wall to hear those few awkward pauses when the person on the other end asks him to repeat what it is that he actually does for a living. In order to minimise risk, David, and his father before him, have always fired a stunt double sandbag through the air to see if it hits the target before they actually shoot themselves. He mentions a few occasions when his sand-filled imposter didn't quite hit the mark as he would have liked.

It's at this point that I ask how exactly the cannon works. I assume that this is going to be a fairly straightforward answer and that some kind of spring mechanism is going to be explained to me. It turns out, however, to be the only blunt point of the entire interview. My request for information about the actual firing mechanism is met with the simple reply that it's our "secret sauce". I know enough about tone to know that we are done, but he does make up for the lack of technical information with an explanation on how he and his father, along with his brother, hand built the very weapon that is essentially their bread and butter.

I discover during my research that in fact the first human cannonballs can be traced back to the late 1800s so it's certainly not a new kind of event. That said, it's the technical advances that have really made it the spectacle it is today. They are all quite a secretive bunch and apparently even the different human cannonballs around the world don't really know exactly how each other's cannons work, given that there are less than ten of these people in existence. What we do know is that they are all handmade and lovingly maintained by a very few select individuals. My best educated guess is that it's some kind of compressed air-firing mechanism, but that's purely speculation and I'm none the wiser than anyone else out there.

It would be easy to only talk about David himself but he is part of a legacy that his father created out of his own imagination a generation ago when he was a young man himself. David's father, who is aptly named David Snr, was an accomplished circus performer and specialised in the trapeze. It was in his role as a catcher for a flying human body that he came up with the idea of becoming a human cannonball. He set many records before handing the torch over to his son, David Jnr. It's such a unique situation to have been in, it almost seems like a bit too much fiction. It's pretty clear that David Jnr has learned everything he needed to know from his dad and then some. From the physics of cannonballing to how to treat people right it's been shared and passed down from the original Bullet Smith himself. David is glowing about his father's influence, but nevertheless, you get the feeling there might have been some tugs-of-war over cannon designs and show concepts.

I enquire about the role his mother played in this whole affair. I picture her as a lady pacing up and down the hallways of the stadiums, unable to cope with the pressure of seeing two of her family members being shot into the sky over decades and decades. David says that his mum has seen it all but takes it all in her stride. She has seen every single member of her family shot out of a cannon at one stage but has so far resisted the experience herself. There is also talk of David's young son, Maverick, taking on the role that's been passed down a generation already. He's not totally keen on the idea but admits it might be hard to stop him given the young boy's already insatiable appetite for adventure.

'He will probably break all my records one day,' he says, although he's not sure what the young boy's mother might think. Speaking of records, David's last one was back in 2013 when he successfully set the record for the highest-ever cannonball shot. It was officially recognised by The Guinness Book of Records but it wasn't without a bit of pre-show nerves, and it's not surprising that he hasn't attempted another record since.

The team at Guinness asked him to be involved in a programme that they were making called *Unleashed*. They chose to shoot the show in the town of Mojave in California due to the fact that it's quite secluded and near certain facilities they needed. Given that they were in the desert the only feasible time for David to do the stunt was 6am when the temperature was lower. Lower, as David discovered, didn't mean much out there and it was, he says, baking hot as they were about to fire up the cannon. It gets back again to how much the temperature and the humidity alter the maths of how the cannon is fired and the move from night to day meant that calculations were going up and down like a yo-yo.

'Being propelled through thick humid air compared to your typical cool, coastal breeze can add or subtract metres to how far you will or won't go. Additionally, I was also required to be shot through a burning ring of fire which was held in place by an

extremely long crane. There were so many factors at play that I found myself being physically sick from the nerves which had never happened before. Luckily the jump went well but it certainly took its toll on me. When I watched the footage back I realised just how far off I was to hitting the centre of the net which was a bit disconcerting. Other than that it was a nice result and I was happy to be involved with the team from Guinness.'

You do have to wonder how long David can keep doing what he does. The years have certainly taken a certain toll on his body. One suspects he has a few good years left in him though. His days, however, of doing 450 shows a year are over; he has recognised the need for downtime in between shows rather than rushing from one to the other. His body just can't repair itself as fast any more.

Being the world's most famous human cannonball has given him and his family a virtual VIP pass all over the world. He even appeared on *America's Got Talent*. For those few weeks he was on air he couldn't walk down the street or through an airport without being recognised. Once his part in the show finished so did the daily recognition, but you get the feeling he prefers it that way. He's a pretty humble guy who just happens to have an amazingly unique job.

He gets excited at meeting celebrities, as do most people, and it's funny when they really want to hear about what it's like to do what he does, and not the other way around. I asked out of interest just who he has met and he reeled off some crazy long list that sounded like the guest list to the Oscars. He was, however, most excited to meet Bill Murray and they had a good conversation about cannonballing. He has certainly led a very unique life full of amazing experiences and he is very appreciative of the good things it's brought to him along the way.

As his kids get older he is starting to focus more on their needs. He encourages their own interests and does whatever he can to help them with their pursuits. When the season finishes they unload the cannon off the back of the rig and head off together to spend time with each other. One of David's daughters is a budding musician and artist so he actually carries a concert piano for her to play and practise on in the back of the trailer. It's a sign of some truly dedicated parenting, lugging a piano around, but that's just the way he rolls, and always has done.

If you ever get the chance to see David in action on his cannon, make sure you do. It becomes even more interesting once you know the man under the helmet. David "The Bullet" Smith is certainly the ultimate showman and typifies the idea that you can do anything you set your mind to in life, no matter how impossible it seems to those around you. He's living proof that you can have success in the most unique of careers but still have success as a father, even if you are flying by the seat of your pants most of the time, quite literally.

"Big cannon, long distance . . . small net"

X
THE CAVE DIVERS

It's often said that as humans we actually know very little about the underwater world that covers almost three quarters of our planet. It's one of those throwaway lines you'll hear now and then. It's not totally true though. In fact, the entire ocean floor has been mapped by satellite. But this knowledge doesn't extend to the huge number of caves that wind their way underneath the ground we walk over. In fact, some remote caves have been seen by less people than have been to the moon.

Cave diving is a pursuit that seeks to explore and understand what is really below the surface of these deep, watery, black holes that appear all over the world. Underwater caves come in all shapes and sizes. They could be hundreds of miles inland from the ocean and be filled with freshwater or exist very close to the coast and be connected to the ocean, thus affected by tides and currents, just like the open ocean. They tend to appear mostly in limestone rock and can be hundreds of thousands to several millions of years old.

Cave diving has been called one of the deadliest pursuits, but much of that reputation is a touch unjustified. It's true that deaths occur in the sport annually, but fatalities are generally down to lack of cave diving training. When experienced divers die, more often than not those deaths are caused by the divers breaking their own golden rules of exploration. Divers will often find themselves five hundred feet below the surface, with no natural light and only a guide line to lead them back to safety.

Unlike ocean diving, where one has the option in an emergency to rise straight to the surface, with cave diving there is no rip cord you can pull. It takes at least the same amount of time to get out as it takes to get in.

GRANT PEARCE

Grant Pearce, the first of two subjects in this chapter, is a world-renowned cave diver with some thirty-five years experience. Considering he is only 56 years old he's actually been doing it much longer than he hasn't been doing it. As a young boy, it was watching Jacques Cousteau's old films that hooked him on exploring. Since then, he's been to some of the deepest, darkest and scariest depths of the earth that any man has ever visited and lived to tell the tale.

Although cave diving is not his full-time job, he's kind of become what you might call a hired gun. There are only a handful of people in the world who can do what he does, which is why he gets invited sometimes by governments to explore newly found caves around the world. He was fortunate enough, for example, to be invited as one of four hand-picked specialist cave divers to join an exploration trip to the Cook Islands, whose caves are some ten million years old. The mission was funded by the Cook Island Tourist Board who paid the group to explore as many cave diving locations on their island as they could possibly do in four weeks and then report back on the potential for the Cook Islands to become a cave diving destination. On another occasion he found himself immersed in the caves of *Piccaninnie Ponds*, which are perhaps Australia's most famous cave diving sites.

He was, he says, lucky in life to discover something that really mattered to him, and even luckier to find a woman to share it with in wife, Lynne. After the birth of their children, Emma and Aaron, the pair inevitably made the move from the Barossa Valley to Mt Gambier in South Australia where they could be closer to the best caves in the country, and soon after they built a dive lodge which was and continues to be a Mecca for backpackers interested in cave diving on their travels.

Lynne made the unprompted choice not to dive any more once the children had been born. In some ways, he says, it's sad that he no longer gets to go on underwater adventures with his best dive buddy, but at the same time he has never lost sight of the personal sacrifice she made for the benefit of their family.

Once you really get your head around the real dangers of the sport it's pretty easy to understand why some people might choose to discontinue it once a family comes along. As Grant explains you can in some ways never truly relax and never ever forget the golden rules. If you ever sprained an ankle back in high school you'll remember the coach or teacher telling you the R.I.C.E. technique which stands for **R**est, **I**ce, **C**ompression and **E**levation. Cave divers have their own mnemonic and they repeat the mantra…The **G**ood **D**ivers **A**lways **L**ive which stands for Training, Guidelines, Depth, Air supply, Lights. It's vital to follow if you intend to dive another day.

Without a doubt the most dangerous aspects of cave diving are the cave divers themselves and the capacity to know their own limits. How to problem-solve and handle potential stressful situations and to plan for any situation that could equate to a bad day in the office. Low to zero water visibility conditions are an everyday occurrence during most cave dives.

In order to navigate their way around the caves, the divers carry guide lines on reels or small spools, either left in the cave by prior dive teams or laid out by the divers themselves. The guide line provides a continuous link to the surface and is carefully laid along the way by wrapping it around protruding rocks. It's not a totally foolproof method, however. Divers at the back of the pack could dislodge a line, or the rock itself could dislodge and cause a break in the line, but these kinds of things are the things that one always needs to be prepared for. Much of the skill of diving is to be able to remain calm in the event that one loses visual and or tactile contact with the cave line.

By far and away the most dangerous part of the sport is when people with only scuba certification, attempt to try cave diving with no cave diving training or without the skills and the correct equipment. Over thirty years ago in Australia so many sea divers were dying in caves that the authorities of the time almost closed down the fledgling sport. Fortunately the numbers of deaths have seriously decreased since regulation was introduced and has been key to the growth of the sport.

Grant respects the risks of cave diving and is all too aware that being in the wrong state of mind can easily lead to accidents. *'I often say to myself, "Are you sure you want to do that today, or push through on this dive? Why not just sit it out and have a go later when it feels right".'*

So each dive is planned and managed in minute detail. He tries to visualise every dive he's about to do and assess the various risk scenarios and responses in his head.

'I always intend to return to the surface after having an awesome time doing what I love, but more so seeing my family at the end of the day.'

Grant has also had the grave misfortune of losing a close friend – and experienced diver – to a cave diving accident. He doesn't want to discuss the details of the incident out of respect for the family but says that essentially something went wrong on her dive and she ran out of air. The tragedy was made all the more real by the fact that Grant was a member of the rescue team who had to go down and recover her body.

His children grew up mixing with cave diving folk and benefitted from socialising with interesting people who come from all over the world to dive at the lodge they ran. Grant says that for him the dangers are really no different than being aware of the risks when driving a car in traffic. He adds though, that a number of close friends cited family as a reason for taking a backward step from the sport as their priorities changed. Some have come back to it, he says, as the children have gotten older, and some haven't. It's really just a personal choice for the individual. I ask him if he thinks his children worry about what he does, given that they have both dived and understand implicitly the dangers and what's involved. They know he does not take unnecessary risks, he replies.

'I always go in with a strict plan and follow it, no matter what. If the risk starts to outweigh the plan then I'll exit the dive, no matter how exciting it is. There is definitely an inbuilt cut-off switch in me that has been highlighted since I had Emma and Aaron, and that's what keeps me in check. I'm not willing to leave my kids without their dad. There is no hole in the ground worth dying for and I'm prepared to wriggle out of a hole backwards if that's what it takes to get back to safety.'

As a back up he makes sure he has diver's insurance. In the event of a tragedy there will be enough money to pay off the house and employ someone to clear up the clutter of diving gear that clogs up the shed and lounge room.

You have to marvel a bit about the guy's sense of humour but at the same time you know that everyone in the Pearce family doesn't have any misconceptions about what they are all embroiled in. When you get as good as Grant has become in what can only be described as an obscure sport, every now and then certain spoils will present themselves. Several years back he was approached to be a technical support diver in the Hollywood blockbuster, *Sanctum*, which was filmed in Australia and produced by James Cameron. The plot in some ways was a little like what you might call a lost-in-space type adventure, except it was underwater.

'The experience was eye-opening, to say the least. It was in some ways like a circus production unfolding with all the logistics, equipment, support staff, minders, actors, food, gear, tents, generators and lighting at each site. It was essentially a movie stage above and below ground, with underwater communication equipment, stunt doubles, support crew and actors listening to instructions from the producers. It was amazing to be paid well to supervise something that is essentially a part of who I am. In many ways it made me think about myself as that wide-eyed boy that I was as a teenager who dreamed of following adventure wherever it took me, and here I was in the thick of the mix of a big budget film. It still seems totally surreal even years later.'

Over the years, Grant has also been in some fairly precarious situations himself. Even the most experienced divers can lose their way at times and that is sometimes caused by marvelling at the surroundings of new caves and simply not paying attention. He has, he says, been some seven hundred and fifty metres into an unexplored cave in the Nullarbor Plains in Southern Australia, back in 2011 when he lost concentration for a moment and unintentionally swam into a small side passage, losing sight of both the guide line and his dive buddy. The key to that situation, he says, was that he didn't panic. He deployed his emergency cave reel (it jammed but he managed to get it operational), and thankfully managed to find his bearings again. It was the first time he had ever had to deploy such a line and it came only one month after his close friend perished, so he says it was especially hard to stay calm given what he had seen her family go through.

Cave divers have to fit themselves into some pretty small spaces to get where they are going, which adds a touch of claustrophobia to the whole affair. Grant recalls running into trouble on a dive of an unexplored cave in the Cook Islands. On the ascent he became partially wedged, making this one of the harder ascents he's ever had to do. This is where cave diving gets really serious and you have to really know your stuff in order not to panic.

PROFESSOR TOM ILIFFE

Professor Tom Iliffe is the second cave diver in this chapter. At the age of seventy, he is what can only be described as the grand master of cave diving as he's been doing it for nearly forty-five years. When he first started his career it wasn't even something that anyone really did as a job, and that is an amazingly remarkable thing to say about your life's work. His mug shot on the Texas A&M University website is the first thing that grabs me. It sort of appears as if he's just rushed in from "somewhere" and is struggling to sit still long enough to get the picture taken before he darts back out of the room on the way to his next adventure. He is also vastly experienced and although he has well and truly lost count of the dives he has done he expects that the number is in the thousands.

Tom's career started back in 1977 when he finished his PhD in Marine Biology and was sent to his first job as a research scientist at the Bermuda Biological Station. Prior to that, he tells me that his main interest had been exploring and diving in caves but it was strictly as a hobby. When he arrived in Bermuda, he was astonished to find that within a fifteen-minute ride from his house there were well over one hundred caves that had never been fully explored. Many of these caves contained deep, clear blue pools of water that fluctuated with the tides, thus confirming their connection to the sea. Intrigued and excited, he enquired if anybody had ever looked for animals in these caves. His boss replied that a few years before several biologists had ventured into a handful of caves but didn't find a single living thing and decided the cave pools were lifeless, abiotic environments. To Tom, this just didn't seem logical, so he took it on as a personal challenge to see what might really be living down there.

It turns out that there was indeed quite a bit down there and over his stellar career Tom discovered two hundred and fifty new species of marine and freshwater cave dwelling invertebrates from caves around the world. It isn't quite as easy as it sounds, as these sometimes near-microscopic critters inhabit only the deepest, darkest depths. Given the lack of sunlight and limited food supply, nothing grows too big in these parts, so you need your wits about you to try and catch anything that moves. Tom is clearly hooked on cave diving and you do wonder what will become of him if he can no longer do it. He's also quick to explain the reasons why he finds the pursuit so addictive.

'There are many reasons why I enjoy cave diving. It's very serene and peaceful to be weightless in such an environment and

you take in amazing views. From a professional viewpoint, I find that cave diving provides a view into the past whereby I can discover new life forms from surroundings unchanged and untouched for thousands of years. I can be the first person to enter a cave and see these sights, something that is virtually impossible to do anywhere else on the planet.'

He has carved out what you might call a dream job at the university where he is able to ply his trade with his eager students. It must be quite unusual, I think, to have a professor who teaches the theory of an activity and then jumps into a wetsuit and carries on with its practical applications. He seems very mild-mannered to talk to but there seems to be a bit of a dual personality going on with him and you can tell that once he changes out of his "Clark Kent" teaching clothes he morphs into someone a little more edgy.

His job at the university is teaching Biospeleology (a fancy way of saying Cave Biology), Scientific Diving and Tropical Marine Ecology. His Biospeleology course at the university also involves weekend field trips to dry caves in Austin and San Antonio, Texas, and a week-long trip to Arkansas. Let's just say, he doesn't struggle to fill classes. The training he puts them through is very rigorous, and it has to be. He has to make sure that if anyone gets into trouble that they are able to still stay calm and navigate their way out of danger.

One of the big challenges of cave diving is managing your gas supply. While Tom often utilises side-mount diving (carry a scuba tank under each arm, rather than the standard methods of carrying tanks on your back) to perform dives, he is also a keen exponent of using rebreathers, or what you could call closed circuit systems. These types of systems effectively recycle any breathing gas you exhale back into the system where carbon dioxide is absorbed by special filters and then oxygen added as required. This means that no gases are released into the environment – meaning no bubbles. It's an extremely useful system in that the absence of bubbles helps prevent any silt around you from becoming stirred up, which decreases visibility. It also means that you can dive for a heck of a lot longer which is especially handy when exploring unknown caves where the end point is unknown. Tom says his longest dive with one of these systems was approximately five hours.

Like many of the men involved in this book he doesn't see what he does as particularly dangerous, although he admits that in the past there have been many deaths from the sport, especially years ago when it was in its infancy. He says that up until training programmes were properly developed, some five hundred deaths occurred in Florida caves alone, most all of which were down to inexperience. Tom has dived to depths of four hundred and fifty feet and penetrated more than a mile into submerged caves. He's also had his fair share of close calls, and recounts the time in Mexico, back in 1997, when an underwater avalanche destroyed his guideline and stirred up so much silt that visibility was absolutely zero.

'It's one of those situations that you can't really plan for,' he says, 'but you have to rely on your skills and training to get you through. As it turns out I was lucky to get out of that particular disaster, but the unpredictability of Mother Nature is simply a part of the pursuit. If you go diving long enough, bad things will eventually happen.'

While most caves that Tom explores start on land many do eventually connect to the ocean at some point, even if it's only in an indirect way. This means that they can be heavily influenced by ocean tides. He admits to once getting the tide calculation wrong in a dive in the Bahamas in 2000 and having to pull his way, hand over hand out against the incoming tide to get back to the surface.

Cave divers generally follow the *Thirds* rule when it comes to air supply. One third to get you in, one third to get you out and one third to get you and your dive buddy out in case something goes wrong. So you can see while there is room to compensate for error the margin to recover is still small. A worst-case scenario would be if you or your dive buddy had a total air failure at maximum distance into the cave, the two of you would have to swim out on only one set of tanks.

Both these close calls came at a time when his son, Thomas, was still very young, and he admits that since those incidents he had certainly become even more aware of the consequences if something should go as wrong.

As with cave diving, the logistics of getting back to the surface from a long dive are not much different from deep sea diving as they both require the diver to stop periodically on the way back up to the surface in order to prevent decompression sickness, which most people know as the bends. Simply put, the pressure of gases such as nitrogen or helium in the diver's lungs and body tissues increases as they dive to greater depths. The compression of these gases means they absorb into the tissue of the body but are not utilised or expelled. The only way they can be released from the body safely is to allow them to release naturally as the diver slowly makes his way to the surface with periodic stops every ten feet. This isn't a fast process, though, and can take many hours. While it's usually a fairly peaceful process, if you've just experienced a near miss or tragedy in a cave, it can make it harder not to want to get to the surface as quickly as possible. This is where Tom says that the ability to keep calm and composed can mean the difference between success and serious injury including paralysis or even death.

He also has plenty of amazing stories that seem a bit like they could be out of the pages of an adventure book. He tells me about one of his most memorable dives…

'One of the strangest caves I've explored is on Lanzarote in the Canary Islands. While most of the caves we dive in are made from limestone, this one was created in volcanic rock. These caves or tunnels are naturally formed by flowing lava which moves beneath the hardened surface. Such lava tubes drain molten lava from a volcano during an eruption and can remain after the volcano has become extinct, meaning the lava flow has ceased and the rock has

cooled and left a long cave just below the surface of the ground. The lava cave on Lanzarote starts at the base of a volcano in the middle of the island and actually extends out underneath the sea floor of the Atlantic. It's called the Atlantida Tunnel – literally meaning the tunnel to Atlantis. I had to remind myself where I was exactly when I was effectively surrounded by rock that originated from deep underneath the Earth's crust. It felt in some ways as if I was making a journey to the centre of the earth.'

Over his stellar career, as both an educator and a daring pioneer, Tom has managed to quite literally write the book on cave diving. He has co-authored three books, as well as writing close to two hundred and fifty book chapters and journal articles on just about every facet of the pursuit that you could imagine. If he hasn't written about it then it probably isn't worth knowing about.

It's been an interesting mixture trying to write about two cave divers as collectively both men are what is classed as "push divers". They are the ones who are first to jump in the deep end and see what is on the other side. Like deep ocean divers they also know that there are no pre-existing guide lines to the caves they want to explore, and they wouldn't have it any other way. They have both had slightly different experiences in the sport as well, although both are heavily involved in the teaching of the sport which they both do with boundless enthusiasm.

One parallel that I noted throughout our interviews was that they both had very attentive fathers and that adventure was encouraged and nurtured. They have both clearly ignited the fire of adventure in their own offspring. Tom's son, Thomas, is an avid cave diver himself and is always asking his dad to be taken on dives wherever he goes. They have a fantastic father/son relationship and Tom always obliges when he can. He also includes Thomas' wife, Ashlee, who has also been infected by the cave-diving bug. Grant's children, Emma and Aaron, are also go-getters. Emma is a qualified boat handler and budding scientist, and Aaron flew a plane by the time he was sixteen, as well as both being very competent divers.

So, what do we have? Two extraordinary dads (plus the mums of course) and a bunch of extraordinary kids! I noted to myself at the close of the interviews that it was a shame that these two men from opposite sides of the globe had never met given that they both exist in the upper echelons of the sport. I penned a very simple message to them both which simply read…

'Tom, please meet Grant. You guys should go diving together sometime.'

"Journey to the centre of the world"

XI
THE BODYGUARD

It's going to be difficult to write about a bodyguard. That's the realisation I have well before the start of my search to find one even begins. It's a profession we think we know everything about when actually we know very little. It's a career shrouded in a fair portion of mystique as well as elements of secrecy and anonymity, aspects which are going to be tough to try and work around.

That's before we even discuss confidentiality. People pay vast sums of money hiring bodyguards to protect them, and all sorts of legal documentation needs to be signed before they can begin. Even if the piece is written with total anonymity, aspects still have to be changed to ensure that the clients are unable to recognise any part of themselves in the story.

George Foster is a bodyguard and a Group Managing Director for a company called *Intelligent Protection International Limited*, based in the UK. You can't help but slightly fall prey to your expectations of what a bodyguard should look and sound like, and after he sends me a family picture so I can get a better feel for who he is, the stereotype is debunked a little on both accounts. He is extremely articulate and very well spoken where I had perhaps expected a slightly gruff, less talkative kind of guy who has been hardened by years of hard and stressful work. He's also nothing like I thought he'd look like. While he's certainly a good-looking chap, he isn't a colossal muscle-bound man by any means, although you can tell he is fit. He looks pretty normal really, the kind of guy you might see in a bar or walking down the street who looks much like anyone else. We later learn a bit more about why appearances are very important in some aspects of his work, and why being able to blend in with a crowd is often an essential attribute – but I'll get to that later.

Initially George schools me on certain terms in the industry. Not clients, but "the principal", for example. He refers to himself as working in "close protection security" rather than being a "bodyguard", a term that is slightly outdated for those in the industry.

Falling foul of the industry's much-loathed stereotypes is actually fairly easy to do and only requires a passing comment of the aforementioned Hollywood blockbuster, *The Bodyguard*.

So, is it true? Would he dive in front of his client/principal and take a bullet to save their lives? The answer itself is actually no, but definitely not for the reasons you might think. He says it's most definitely a question he's been asked before, so he's well versed in explaining the logic behind the answer. Essentially, he explains that if you get to a point where you are having to put yourself in front of your principal to save them from a bullet, then you are certainly already too late.

'If someone is taking aim with a weapon at my principal, be it a gun or a knife, the chances are very high that if I make the heroic movie-star dive in front of the travelling bullet or the thrust of a blade, that there will be a second bullet ready to be fired at your principal. Perhaps even a second, third and fourth thrust of a blade aimed at them after you have been removed from the situation.'

The point, he explains, is that no matter if an assailant is intent on killing, maiming or embarrassing your principal, they will always display physical, behavioural indicators that he and his fellow operatives can't afford to miss.

Without wanting to sound too analytical on his behalf, if you research historic assassination attempts they show (with possibly the exception of the JFK assassination) that more often than not, despite the range on some weapons nowadays, most attacks occur from no more than three feet away from the intended target. If someone gets that close with the intent to commit an assault of some sort, or worse still, murder, then the person responsible for them will definitely have missed, somewhere, a crucial indicator of intent from the assailant.

George says he may only have a split second to respond to the realisation of one of these indicators but a second can save a life and allow you to escape and evade. This is why it is imperative to maintain the highest level of concentration at all times because in this specialism they don't get second chances.

He has become quite a master of his craft despite only having been directly involved with it for five years. The transition to it was made a lot easier though, as he has been involved in the security industry in various capacities for the last sixteen years. His clients, or principals as he calls them, come from all walks of life. They include High Net-Worth Individuals, Foreign Royalty/Heads of State, A-list celebrities and general members of the public that have had specific threats made against them. Every principal is different and will always have unique needs; there is no one size fits all plan for protecting them.

I cite for him the famous occurrence in London a few years ago when Tom Cruise was assaulted by an individual posing as a member of the press. He leaned over the barrier to ask him a question and squirted him in the face with water from a fake microphone. Now, of course, no harm was done but Tom certainly lost his cool and it was an embarrassing incident for him, being such a public figure. Perhaps it was a case of Tom's team letting their guard down slightly as he was in an area that was designated for the press, who are typically vetted by security. It turned out that the men behind the stunt were actually working on a TV show for a major television channel so were able to access that area fairly easily. That would no doubt have been a watershed moment for anyone in the close protection industry as a reminder of why it's important to be vigilant at all times.

Those in close protection these days are also there lots of times to prevent humiliation just as much as injury, especially when the person has a certain level of fame. Tom was just very lucky that it was a toy he was assaulted with and not a more serious weapon. Despite being a good example of what can go wrong in celebrity close protection, George chooses not to comment. It seems as if there is a bit of an unwritten rule that, to put it fairly bluntly, you don't stick the boot in.

George initially got into the security industry as a means of gaining experience in order to fulfil his ambition to become a police officer. Serving is somewhat of a tradition in the Foster family. Almost all his family have served at some point in their lives and it was something he felt he might also be good at. However, as time rolled on, he quickly developed a real interest and passion for close protection.

The decision to move into this sector came right around the time that his first child was born. I asked, as I always do, if there was any specific conversation that he and his wife had about the realities and dangers of working in a field, especially now that he had the added responsibility of supporting a young family. He replies that he and his wife certainly had many a lengthy discussion prior to him following his ambition to work in this sector. Dads, he says, undoubtedly can't do what they do without a strong, supportive and extremely understanding partner.

George and his wife are parents to two young boys aged two and six. He certainly doesn't need any other reason than that to come home safely each day, which is why safety and attention to every little detail is so important in his work. There is, of course, the risk of death when you do a job like his. As a result, he has a very extensive life insurance plan should something go wrong, and his family will be well taken care of should anything ever happen to him. It does concern him though, that many younger people in the industry have very basic insurance and no real plan in case of a tragedy. With that in mind, he says, all you can really do is advise these guys and girls accordingly – look after your own interests and that of your family first and foremost.

The job really can be hard on family life. Travelling abroad to undertake contracts means missing out on small parts of your children's lives. Important milestones are often casualties. Kids grow up quickly, and sometimes a week away from home means you have to see or hear something on FaceTime or Skype that you would have much preferred to hear and see in person. While he doesn't have many regrets in life, he does wish that he had followed his dream a little sooner and entered the industry before his sons came along as he feels that this would have let him spend more time with his family.

While there isn't what you'd call a typical day, every task is relentless – as it should be, he states. The days consist of equipment checks, extensive reconnaissance and lots of other prior planning. He is constantly preparing for changes in the principal's itinerary and it's his job to think quickly and adapt and overcome at very short notice. The days also include heavy liaison with the principal's PA, any third-party involvement, driver or drivers, venue security and any applicable authorities. Report writing and threat analysis is also another key part of a standard day. Then, of course, he has the physical carrying out of the job, which could entail taking one's principal to the most extravagant of places one minute and standing in a hotel lobby for endless hours the next. In both cases, one thing must always be constant and that is maintaining the highest level of concentration and awareness of what's going on around them. It's the very minor details that count, and if the assailant shows his hand and he misses it, it puts everyone in potential danger.

While many of his stories are off limits, he does, however, give me one of his own stories that is a fairly good indicator of the average type of day that he encounters. A few years ago he found himself looking after the daughter of a Head of State who had decided to go shopping at a major department store in Central London. The principal was around fifteen or sixteen years of age at the time and very much the apple of her father's eye. About half an hour after entering the store, George noticed a short, slightly scruffy male who looked wholly out of place in this department store. George believed at the time the man had absolutely no idea that he was with the principal because he was maintaining very much a covert presence at the time. He continued watching him and he could see that he was continually looking at the principal, but he had cleverly positioned himself out of her eyesight. As these were indicators that something might be afoot, George approached and advised the principal that it would perhaps be better for them to move on.

George is aware that people may think he's being paranoid but to that he simply says… *'Now some may say, "Well, nothing actually happened", but that is the name of the game, to ensure nothing happens. Being proactive rather than reactive. If you're being reactive then it's already too late and the horse may have bolted. But, if your principal genuinely values why you are there, there will be no problem in getting them to move. So what if nothing happened had we stayed, you might ask? Well, nothing happened when we moved away either.'*

The talk about children being involved in close protection work brings George to speak unprompted about the recent killing of a police officer, PC Keith Palmer, who was also a father, and who was killed in 2017 in the line of duty by a man with a political and religious agenda whilst tying to defend the Houses of Parliament in Westminster, London. It's not a million miles away from what George does himself and, as mentioned earlier, he once had aspirations of becoming a police officer as many of his family members have served in the force. It clearly cut close to the bone and leads us down a very interesting path discussing the fears all fathers experience about the safety of their own family.

You could, as he says, simply be out and about with your own family and find yourself in a compromising situation. I express to him my single biggest fear: to be put in a situation where your family is in danger and you are not able to protect them. It might be being involved in a terrorist attack or facing a possible home invasion. It's the kind of thing that keeps dads awake at night given the state of the world these days. I wanted to know if he has any specific advice he could give your average dad to prepare for any situations that might arise. He has a simple answer: Use your intuitive instinct. *'If you feel there is something not quite right, then you'll find more often than not, it isn't.'*

Bodyguards are primarily thinkers and escape artists, and avoid conflict by using their intuition and ability to see what others don't. Fathers should use the same principles. If alarm bells ring, he says, do not stand and fight unless it's completely unavoidable – just get out of there as fast as you can.

One common misconception about their work is that people expect them to be fighters and be able to take apart a pack of knife-wielding thugs with a few air brush-like moves. While the training he has certainly gives him an essential set of tools and an edge to be able to deal with the assailants trying to inflict harm on himself or his principal, it's always a last resort.

His golden rule is to always give yourself at least two means of escape as often as possible. That could be as simple as just knowing where the fire escapes or the elevators are in a building you've never been in before. It may sound extreme to some but just try it yourself, he says, even for a week. It will become a habit and it will stand you in good stead to survive most situations life can throw at you.

With some vigour he pleads to men never to be fooled into thinking that it's somehow unheroic to fast-track yourself out of there – because it's not. Fear is a very natural and useful emotion, especially if you channel it in the correct way and use it, as opposed to fighting it. In fact, you should embrace fear as it's an incredible design by the human body to let you know something has gone wrong or is about to go wrong. This emotion can help you escape from impending trouble.

George had to go through a very intense training course to get his foot in the door of the world of close protection. He was trained by former Royal Military Police Close Protection Unit and Special Forces personnel. The training itself was crammed into 21 days, each day 13-14 hours long, involving areas such as Medical Training, Law, Reconnaissance, Walking Drills, Car Convoy and Tactical Driving Drills, Reaction to Attack both on foot and in a vehicle, Surveillance Awareness, Close-quarter Combat, Threat & Risk Assessment, Operational Planning and Route Selection. His skills were then honed and developed over time through experience.

Surprisingly, he doesn't, nor has he ever, carried a gun. Having operated and managed projects in several countries now he's never felt the need to recommend the carrying of a gun, nor has it been a requirement from any of his principals to carry a weapon of any sort.

'For me, the devil is in the detail and ninety-nine percent of close protection is planning for every eventuality and ultimately avoiding the use of a firearm. We don't just have a plan A & B; we have a plan from A, right through to Z. If you have reason to draw a firearm, the chances are you have already missed a vital indicator of intent somewhere and it may already be too late.'

You can't talk to a bodyguard in this period of time without asking his opinion on the infamous robbery that involved Kim Kardashian in an apartment block in Paris. It's the kind of situation that George may have to experience one day, so it's intriguing to get his thoughts. Interestingly her bodyguard, Pascal Duvier, was actually not at the apartment the night of the robbery. He is also a fairly high-profile figure himself with close to seventy-five thousand Instagram followers. He seems in direct contrast to George who has this to say on the subject: commenting on another close protection worker is, as mentioned before usually off limits, and seen as bad form. However, as the Kardashian case was so high-profile George is happy to give his thoughts.

'In my humble opinion, the work of a Close/Executive Protection Operative is to blend in and very much be the "grey man". I fear, in this particular instance, that Pascal perhaps may have got distracted from what he was actually there to do. His use of social media was very poor and actually may have contributed in part to the blueprint of this attack. It's in a sense a good example of brains being called into action before brawn. Whilst a man mountain like Pascal may serve a terrific purpose for navigating his principal through a crowd or a hotel entrance "the thinker" will have had his principal out the back door, in a normal vehicle, ten minutes after a prestige decoy vehicle has gone, complete with an imposter principal. Obviously, the Kardashians are unique clients and probably cause their minders many headaches, so it's difficult to be too judgemental,' he says.

What's been established here though, is that George has a very steady head on his shoulders. He's now set on a path to take his career as far as it can go, and there is little doubt he will succeed. He speaks highly of his colleagues, and the family who supports him through his work. He was, as he says, very lucky to have a strong father figure himself and it's something he's keen to provide for his own boys.

For my last question to close the interview, I decide to give the Hollywood stereotype one more outing. I ask him how he feels about people's misconceptions about bodyguards always dying first or perhaps simply being used as bullet catchers in the movies.

'It's because they have never read the chapter in this book,' he says with a smile.

"Brains , Braun and lightening reflexes"

XII
THE KNIEVEL

©Buster McWhorter

If you wanted to witness the true definition of an alpha male and how he behaves, the best place to look would be the animal kingdom. And by far and away the easiest species in which to see this trait is the lion, which has always been king of the jungle. Within a pride of lions there is always a dominant male that rules the pack, having earned the right to do so through what was probably a ferocious battle and victory with the previous ruler of the pride. It is, however, an extremely difficult mantle to hold onto as he is under constant, but not always noticeable, pressure to keep his position as top dog.

The defining characteristic of a lion alpha male can be witnessed when the pride is at rest after a day of hunting. Spread out in small groups the lions lie resting or licking their wounds inflicted by the chase of the kill. What's interesting is that during this time the dominant males never ever make eye contact with any of the other males. To do this would be seen as a sign of weakness in that they are admitting that they perceive them as a threat and therefore have to watch their movements. While the concept might be a little different in our world the same principles apply to those extreme sportsmen who lead the pack. They don't follow or copy; they set the boundaries as they go along.

Robbie Knievel is one of the greatest motorbike jumpers of all time, and maybe still is, depending on who you ask. While he is of course the son of Evel Knievel, who is considered perhaps the godfather of extreme sports. Robbie was actually a more successful jumper by quite some margin. As it's been said before about the pair – Evel broke bones; Robbie broke records.

Robbie had somewhat of an auspicious entry into the world in that his father was actually in jail when his mother, Linda, gave birth to him. The early years of his life were basically an apprenticeship in dangerous activities. By the time he was eight he was regularly featuring in his father's shows, at times even stealing his father's thunder. How often do you see a small boy pop an endless wheelie in front of a crowd, with effortless ease like he was shelling peas? Robbie spent his early years in Butte, Montana riding his BMX over the biggest jumps he could find. When you're the son of Evel Knievel there really isn't any other option. He recalls the very moment during one of his dad's shows on a football field in Toronto when, as an eleven-year-old, he knew it was what he wanted to do. There was something about the spectacle and the noise of the crowd as his dad jumped that hooked him and he has never really looked back

The daredevil part of Robbie's personality seems to have been hardwired into his brain from birth, and therefore did not need to be cultivated by his father or anyone else. So determined was he to succeed and put himself in harm's way that his mother actually admitted there were times when she didn't know what to do with him.

It certainly wasn't easy for Robbie being the son of a world famous daredevil. Evel, it's said, was unable to compartmentalise his life, and whether he was performing his stunts or sitting in an armchair at home he was always Evel Knievel. Both of them were extraordinarily headstrong and stubborn, making up their own rules as they went along.

Robbie and Evel's relationship was complex. They were the only two people who really understood each other because they had lived the same life and yet they didn't know how to communicate effectively. Evel knew exactly what Robbie would go through getting on that motorcycle and dealing with fears, fans and all the pressures and expectations that go with that. Robbie in turn understood what his dad went through getting to where he did as he saw first-hand all the crashes, and watched all those bones heal one day at a time.

Unfortunately, however, they never really saw eye to eye on a lot of things, to the extent that Robbie was handed a few good beatings over the years. Robbie laments that was just his dad's way of trying to do the right thing; best take a stick to the kid rather than lose him to the devil, as he puts it. Family members inform me that they loved each other but that the chemistry between them never mixed, and there was never quite enough space in the room for two egos that size. Given the sometimes harsh nature of the relationship it would be easy for Robbie to be bitter about parts of his upbringing, but he never is. He has always been the biggest man in the room when it came to that and everyone close to him knows it.

Time, they say, is a great healer. It's been almost a decade since Evel Knievel died. You can tell that Robbie has accepted the relationship for what it was and has become self-aware enough to realise he perhaps contributed to the sometimes dysfunctional nature of their relationship just as much as his father did.

Back on New Year's Eve 1967, when his father jumped the fountains at Caesars Palace, Robbie just couldn't comprehend how he had even come up with the idea of trying something like that. Since then, Robbie's always felt privileged to be a part of ground-breaking events. Robbie was only five years old then and after that always felt like he had to live up to the reputation of being the son of Evel Knievel. He out-jumped every kid in their little town and broke countless pushbikes doing it, but that's just what he felt he had to do.

Then there was the fame.

'It was pretty strange when my dad signed the toy deal at the height of his fame in 1973 and all of a sudden he was an action figure that you could buy in the toy store. It even outsold GI Joe. That's how popular it was at the time, although it never outsold Barbie which was something that my dad and I found pretty funny. I also ended up getting my own Robbie Knievel action figure; it never sold anything like my dad's but it's pretty cool looking back on that. I don't think there are very many people that can say they have been for sale on toy shelves.'

Robbie has always had to live in his dad's shadow even after he stopped jumping and it took him a long time to accept this. Every guy wanted to know him and every woman wanted to be with him, but it was difficult as a teenager trying to follow in his footsteps, and trying to deal with everything that came with it.

Evel was known to hate the fact that his son was a heavy drinker even though he had learned it from him, and that he partied endlessly and dabbled in drugs. Evel was a true showman in every sense of the word. He hated being late or cancelling a jump for any reason whatsoever; disappointing his fans was not an option. Robbie was a bit more fastidious about his preparations and would only jump if everything was as it should be. Relatives recall his father freaking out in a motor home one time at one of Robbie's jumps because he was making people wait in the heat while he got his game head on for the jump.

You can understand the conflict, but the reality was that Robbie was a smarter jumper than his father and that's evident for many reasons. Firstly, he jumped further, higher and for much longer than his father but he also had a career that has so far spanned twice that of his father's. While Robbie broke plenty of bones, his approach to danger ultimately is the reason he's known as arguably the greatest living jumper. To his credit despite being a tough old screw, Evel would always correct people who said he was the 'greatest daredevil'. That was not true, he would reply. 'Robbie is the greatest daredevil.'

Many scientific studies have proven that people who are genetically hardwired to take risks are also prone to suffer addictions to alcohol and drugs. Robbie started drinking from the age of twelve and lived a flamboyant lifestyle, at least certainly while at the height of his fame in the eighties and nineties. Life was one long party.

Daredevils or risk-takers become hooked on the thrill of danger and often look for ways to replicate that feeling through alcohol and drugs. They also serve to take the edge off what can be a highly stressful life. Perhaps the biggest part of his issues with alcohol was the fact that he was able to drink what can only be described as colossal amounts. He was known to regularly consume up to twelve double whiskies in a single sitting. With the portion sizes in the US, I would hazard a guess that he was taking more than thirty shots a night which is almost a full litre bottle – enough to send most people to hospital. Robbie has recently become sober – he says age caught up with him and he was tired of being hungover – and is now back jumping again at the age of fifty-five. Seems like this old daredevil had been reborn. They say everyone has a different "low" and thankfully he found his before it was too late. He claims he can still jump as well as he ever could even though the body doesn't take a crash like it used to.

'I'm enjoying my life as a grandfather and it's even better now I'm sober. I do have regrets about what happened when the girls were younger and I wish I hadn't partied so much. However, it was just part of who I was and what I did at the time, and it was a difficult aspect of my life to escape. As far as retiring goes, well, they will be disappointed that I have no real plans for that and want to be still jumping so my great grandchildren can watch too! I'm going to keep jumping as long as I can because I know as soon as I walk off the stage there is no coming back on. All the good times and jumps and everything that went along with it will just be a memory.'

Even if he doesn't quite make it to the great-grandfather jumping show rest assured there will be plenty for the next generations of Knievels to look back on.

Robbie had a profound impact on the daredevil world and the extreme sports events that we all know today. He was the first jumper to do hands-free jumps which kind of became his trademark, and he influenced the next generation to push the boundaries even further. He has so far completed some three hundred and fifty serious jumps and is the holder of twenty world records.

In 1989 Robbie successfully jumped the fountains at Caesars Palace in Las Vegas back. His father had tried it in 1967 but broke a number of bones trying, and ended up in a coma for thirty days, or so the story goes. It's hard to describe the horror of that crash but upon impact his body gives the impression it's shattering like glass on the inside when he hits the tarmac. Robbie was there to witness the horror of the crash as a five-year-old but surprisingly it did little to dampen his enthusiasm for the sport. His father's attempt remains to this day the most famous motorbike crash of all time, and it raised the bar of what daredevils would put themselves through for glory.

It was attempted again in 1980 by another rider, but that effort ended in colossal failure too and the rider, Gary Wells, ended up hitting a concrete wall at eighty-five miles per hour. Both riders were lucky to be alive after their accidents, let alone be able to walk. Despite its lavish setting the jump itself is wickedly difficult in that it's not very long, nor in a straight line for that matter. Another immensely dangerous part is the landing which is incredibly short and into a narrow entrance to an underground car park. A couple of degrees, either way, and one could end up on a solid cement wall or a metal pylon. It requires incredible precision.

Robbie's jump was a fairly nervous affair considering the horrific crashes that had come before it. He made quite a number of practice runs leading up to it and you can't help but wonder what on earth was going through his head. He had a wife and a young daughter in the stands as well as millions of viewers watching at home, and the whole thing could have quite easily become a live televised funeral. Luckily the jump was a spectacular success and you can almost hear the crowd sigh with relief. It was a pretty emotional moment for the whole family and obviously a huge achievement for Robbie to complete the jump that his father had never managed.

There were plenty of further heroics after this Las Vegas jump, and in the ten or so years that followed, it saw him jump pretty much anything and everything that they could build a ramp in front of. In one televised jump in 1999 he jumped between two sixteen storey buildings one hundred and thirty feet apart with nothing at the bottom but the sidewalk to land on if it all went wrong. He's been flying off ramps for a mind-numbing forty-eight years and in his career he managed to jump twice as high and twice as far as his dad.

Not all jumps were crowned in success. His jump of the Grand Canyon, for example, ended in probably the most spectacular crash of his career. He made the actual jump itself quite easily but hit a small cactus shortly after landing that sent him slamming into the dirt and colliding with the hay bales at the end of the landing strip. He had agreed with the local native Indians that he wouldn't desecrate the sacred ground by flattening it and he paid a decent price for that promise. He still managed to stand up with a broken leg and thank everyone for coming along to watch – the true showman indeed.

Some of his other more technical stunts were jumping over a car and a train. Thing is though, the train was coming straight at him and the car was mid-air doing the same when he jumped it, given that he had just jumped a ramp as well. Then both the train and the car proceed to smash through the ramp he has just left. It's pretty technical stuff and the timings would only have to be out by a second for something to go badly wrong. The pressure of the timings, he told me, is pretty intense and once you pull on that throttle there is no turning back. Similarly, he says, live television events were also very full on. There were schedules and timings but when they said *action* you had to go, no matter what.

The kind of fame Robbie enjoyed at his peak also presented him with the opportunity to do endorsements as well as bag quite a few television and movie roles. Perhaps one of his most well-known roles was appearing in the very popular *Chips* series, essentially playing himself. It was a decent speaking role and he does it fairly well. Often when you get sports star cameos they tend to be very wooden but it wasn't a bad effort at all considering he really had no acting experience. It's been said, and I think it's fairly accurate, that he didn't have quite the stage presence of his father who would routinely whip crowds into a frenzy before jumps, whereas Robbie was a quieter showman who mainly let his jumping do the talking.

Robbie actually ended up with his own reality TV show in 2005 called *Knievels Wild Ride*. It certainly lived up to its name and it can't have been easy for the film crew to follow around a hard-core group of bikers getting up to all sorts of shenanigans. It only lasted a season and the ratings were okay, but it was just one of those shows that didn't make it for a variety of reasons.

He speaks very candidly about how he can't quite believe he's still alive, and that's not just from the jumping. There's been some stupid stuff too, like drink-driving, which could have killed someone and he's not proud of that. He also robbed a record shop when he was still a teenager and almost ended up in jail. Perhaps, he says, his injuries along the way were God's way of punishing him – the concussions, the broken bones, the torn ligaments and the endless rehab that went with it. In a way he feels like he's paid his dues for the times he was reckless with other people's lives.

Robbie is a father to two daughters. Karmen, now thirty-nine, was born when Robbie was quite young. Although he didn't raise her, the pair are in contact and he is the proud grandfather of her two children, Analise and Kane. He later married his first wife, Lorin, in 1986 and they went on to have a daughter called Krysten. Lorin tells me he showered her with compliments. Quite the good-looking and charming young man, and a fearless and famous daredevil with all the confidence in the world.

Although the marriage was over in three years, Krysten would often attend many of his jumps which she describes in the foreword of this book. She would also sing the National Anthem at the start of many of the shows Robbie featured in. Now thirty-two, she has her own family and has made her father a grandfather again with Chase. I tell Robbie that Krysten has mentioned in our conversations that she wishes he would retire, to which he laughs and says that everyone has been saying that for years, and he has been saying he would retire since the age of twenty-five.

When I ask Robbie about fear, he explains to me that he's able to control the fear of those jumps, but one thing that always plays on his mind is a potential mechanical failure, as it's out of his hands. One simple spark plug failure, seconds before he hits that ramp, would cause enough engine loss to make him fall short of the landing ramp and freefall to his death. The ramps and the distances you see are super-calculated and in the early days of Robbie's career he built them himself with his crew of guys.

He partly jokingly comments that the biggest competitor in life in his profession is death, and I don't doubt that for a second. A single degree in direction or 10mph off the optimum jump speed is enough for it all to end in tragedy.

Robbie is perhaps one of the most resilient men featured in this book. He was there at the very start of it all with his dad as an eight-year-old boy with eyes as wide as saucers. It's amazing to think how far the world of action sports has come, and Robbie essentially became the bridge that took his father's work of the sixties and the seventies and bulldozed it into the new millennium. He's adamant that there was never any other option for him, and it's the only life he ever wanted.

Robbie's last high-profile jump to date was a 200-foot jump over the volcano at the Mirage Hotel in Las Vegas. It was made all the more impressive by the fact that it came four decades after his first. He not only managed to beat his father at his own game in the end but finally managed to beat his own demons as well. He's now fully recharged and jumping at any chance he gets when most guys his age are looking for a comfortable chair to be a mere spectator in the sunset of their lives. His father, Evel, famously had a gravestone made before what he and everyone else thought would be his certain death being propelled over Snake River Canyon in Idaho by way of a rocket. He lived to tell the tale though, and happily posed alongside the rocket with a slight smirk of invincibility on his face and with giant etched letters that said 'EXPLORER', which

I guess was probably the most apt description of the pioneer of modern-day daredevilry.

I decided to ask Robbie, without wanting to tempt fate, how he would like to be remembered and what he would like his tombstone to say. Alluding to the introduction I suggest maybe 'lion tamer' would be very apt?

'Oh, I'm not sure about that,' he says. 'My dad was a pretty big Lion! How about Traveller? Modern Gypsy? The best things in life are free?'

For a man who has rewritten the book on stunt jumping, I suspect he's earned the right to have whatever he wants written. That's what you get when you've been the leader of the pride.

"The jump that started it all"

XIII
THE AQUA MAN

DARING RESCUE BID BY ABALONE DIVER

'A day I will never forget'

Forest abalone diver Phill Critchlow was relieved to be safe at home with his wife and two young children last night.

Earlier in the day he would have found it hard to believe he would ever see them again.

Phill was one of the many Stanley and Smithton fishermen who answered the call to assist distressed lone rower Tony Dicker.

In a daring rescue attempt, Phill put his life at risk to try to save Stanley fisherman Patrick Hursey when his fishing boat, Moya Anne, capsized while taking part in the rescue operation.

Phill said it was a day he will never forget.

When Phill received the call early in the morning, he readied his 15 m boat, Albatross, and sailed to the rescue site.

He said he could see the rowing shell but couldn't see a body near it.

He was only a few feet from the rowing shell but visibility was poor and fog made it difficult to see anything.

Phill said heavy seas made manoeuvring difficult and the Albatross could not get close to the rowing shell.

During the operation, disaster struck another Smithton fishing vessel, the Moya Anne.

"The sea hit it and she tipped over," Phill said.

"It was just bad luck. She was a good craft and the crew were experienced."

The Albatross was quite close to the Moya Anne when it overturned but Phill could not manoeuvre his boat to get closer.

He saw Patrick Hursey in the water in distress and without thinking he pulled off his gumboots, jumped into the water and started swimming to him.

"He was 30 yards away when I jumped in. But I just couldn't get to him in time. When I last saw him he was about 20 yards away from me. He just went under and didn't come back up again.

"The worst part was being so close and not being able to get him."

Phill does not believe he acted bravely. He dismissed talk of his actions with the comment, "I couldn't sit here now if I hadn't jumped over the side."

The Moya Anne's other crewman, Peter Brown, was trapped briefly in the engine room before he was pulled from the water and taken to the Smithton General Hospital and admitted for observation.

Last night he was reported to be in a satisfactory condition.

Yesterday's experiences have left Phill in no doubt that adventurers who want to test themselves against the Bass Strait should be told from the beginning that they will be on their own.

"They will get no assistance from us again," Phill said.

"This is not the first time it has happened and we are tired of idiots who expect people to go out after them.

"We don't mind when it is in the course of earning our livelihood but not when it is to go after someone following a hare-brained scheme.

"I wouldn't have gone to Melbourne yesterday in my 30-footer, yet two runabouts and three fishing boats were called out to assist in the search for a rowing shell.

"People have to learn to have respect for the Bass Strait. She's the boss and they are tough waters."

Phill Critchlow safely at home last night with his children, Zeb (6) and Kelly (15 months).

As far as our existence goes on planet Earth there are really only two experiences that are totally guaranteed – one is life and the other is death. Unfortunately, it remains unknown for everyone how much time will elapse between the two. The newest of arrivals might get the chance to take only a few gasps of air after they are born before their time is up, or they might live on to walk a billion steps.

There is, of course, that grey area involving near-death experiences where people claim to have put one foot on the other side but have come back and continued living. During that time, depending on the severity of their experience, most, if not all, of their vital signs disappear. They stop breathing, their heart stops beating and they can in some cases flatline. There are countless tales of near-death experiences where people have recalled floating out of their body and looking down upon themselves or being pulled through a tunnel towards a bright light. Whether you believe in the afterlife or not, this chapter is about a guy who believes he had the kind of near-death experience that people speak about. It happened a very long time ago when he was just a young boy but the event went on to shape the rest of his life.

Phil Critchlow is a sixty-five-year-old retired diver from Tasmania, Australia who resides in a rugged west coast town called Marrawah with his wife, Audrey. The town itself is a bit of a "blink and you'll miss it" affair. It's a short strip of road with a shop at one end and a pub at the other as well as a telephone box somewhere in the middle.

Phil's main career was as an abalone diver (abalones are sea snails), which he pursued from the age of eleven, but that didn't quite seem to do justice to his vault of life experiences. The title that stuck in the end was that of the Aqua Man, not because he has gills, well, at least not that we know of, but because his entire life has revolved around the oceans.

He's a warm person to meet in real life but he's been hardened by the elements over the years and has an air of the old invincible sea captain about him. Life for Phil as a young boy wasn't really what you'd call idyllic. His father, he says, was extremely hard on him from the age of seven. He was set the kind of tasks on the family farm that would verge on the lines of slave labour in this day and age. He says that a solid beating was handed out if the work wasn't done, which was often as he was just not capable of doing some of the tasks given his age and strength. He also struggled with his parents' religious beliefs, specifically with the hypocrisy of what was inflicted by the back of his father's hand – sometimes just as he left the Sunday service – when compared to what was preached in church. Aged sixteen, he left the family of his own accord. The local reverend was incensed and told him to never contact his family again unless it was on business matters. Sadly, the relationship never really recovered.

Having developed a fierce work ethic, he was determined to make it on his own. He had, by the age of seventeen, purchased a boat and was totally immersed, quite literally, in the world of abalone diving. He was also totally financially self-sufficient, something that is almost unheard of in this day and age for such a young boy.

To set the scene for Phil's near-death experience, he had recently wrecked the first boat he had bought and was working on another vessel with borrowed diving gear from a friend in order to make money to survive. One particular day during a trip over a shallow sandbar that boat also sank, although, luckily Phil and the crew were able to swim to safety. Unfortunately, with this accident, he lost the diving gear that he had borrowed from a friend. The next day a hastily arranged salvage dive was orchestrated and he spent the day going back and forth from the boat to the seabed trying to retrieve the missing gear. It was imperative that the gear was recovered, as back in the sixties and early seventies diving gear was incredibly hard to source and not just bought in a diving shop like it is today. On about the fourth dive down to the bottom the hose snapped and he found himself on the bottom of the ocean with no oxygen.

In that moment he decided that he really didn't want to fail as he was trying to impress the guys he was diving with. He also didn't want to lose his friend's weight belt which he had had to remove to have any chance of getting back to the surface. With virtually no air left in his lungs he hurriedly attached the hose to the weight belt and let it drop, knowing it could be pulled up later. By the time he had done all that, he had totally expended his oxygen and energy and had given up any chance of making it to the surface.

He jokingly recalls a pod of dolphins swimming around him as he was drowning. Having watched the TV show, *Flipper*, he was certain that they were going to try and help him to the surface. That, of course, didn't happen, and they just looked at him a little puzzled and never came within less than a few metres, shattering the myth. Unable to get to the surface, he eventually blacked out and took in water as his body bobbed around just below the surface. What followed for him, he says, was a very vivid experience involving what he believes was a journey to the other side. Almost fifty years have passed since his experience, and the memory of it remains crystal clear as if it happened yesterday...

'The last thing I remember before I blacked out was feeling as if I wasn't going to make it out alive. Eerily, though, I felt calm and was simply resigned to whatever was about to take place. I suddenly found myself standing in front of a female figure. She was wearing long white robes and asked me simply, "Did I really want to come here"? I laughed at her because I figured I had no say in the matter. Behind her there were thousands of people with very blank expressions staring at me through these old rusty gates, and I remember feeling distinctly uneasy and unwelcome in the whole dimly-lit place.

Although it's hard for Phil to actually recall the order of events, at some point his life did *literally* flash before his eyes, but in a way that is really hard to describe in words.

'It was like a big book and the pages were flicking in my head but I could stop it and look at the pages like hitting the pause button on a movie. Every day of my life was in that book, working backwards from seventeen until I was a baby and could hear myself crying. My life didn't actually flash before my eyes like you hear

about in near-death experiences, it just flowed, and in retrospect made me realise that your brain actually records every moment of your life.'

Then, almost as soon as it started, it was over and all of a sudden he felt himself being pulled back to the surface. His mates in the boat looked over the edge and could just see his hands above his head, floating around lifelessly, only about a metre from the surface. One guy grabbed another guy's ankles and lowered him over the side and they pulled Phil out. They weren't too sure if he was alive or dead but they slung him over the gunwale. Phil then proceeded to empty his stomach of a large volume of saltwater. Because he had not been without oxygen for very long, being dragged over the side of the boat helped drain the water out.

'Looking back, it was a pretty profound experience for a seventeen-year-old to have, but I think in some ways it made me pretty fearless in life and charge head first into doing exactly what I wanted to do from that day on.'

It was after this experience that Phil's passion for diving and his insatiable work ethic really took off. In 1978, ten years after his near-death experience, he moved to Tasmania where the abalone industry was just starting to take off. Tasmania at that stage was a bit of an unexplored wilderness with the kind of underwater bounty that was almost unimaginable in other parts of the world.

Phil had two children in his first marriage, a boy called Zeb and then later, a girl called Kelly. Unfortunately, the marriage came under a bit of a strain in the mid-eighties and both parents went their separate ways with the two children going to live with their mother. Phil still feels twinges of guilt about the separation and the effect on his children. To take his mind off things, he totally immersed himself in his diving. In short time he became a bit of a trailblazer, and it wasn't long before other divers cottoned on to successful catches and began encroaching on his territory.

There is an unwritten rule in the abalone diving world that states that you shouldn't come within one hundred metres of another diver, but not everyone obeyed that rule. He says that he has had three proper punch-ups underwater defending his territory and won all three. Much better than violence though, he found, was to take off the regulator or mask of the encroaching diver and not give it back. That seemed to do the job, he tells me with a laugh. He has lived through the boom days of the abalone industry which was akin to an underwater gold rush, with divers easily earning AUD$ 1,000 a day – an obscene amount of money at the time. He recounts the odd champagne party over the years when they were all virtually underwater rock and roll stars.

Abalone diving is different from most fishing that goes on at sea as it can really only be done by hand. You have a simple knife that you use to pry the abalone shell off the rock and put as many in a bag as you can and return them to the surface before repeating the whole process over again. You soon learn, he says, that you have to almost sneak up on them. Abalones have evolved quite a sophisticated defence and can, it is believed, hear you breathing and see you coming. They also have the ability to clamp their shells even tighter to the rock when they sense danger, which makes it very hard to prise them off.

Time rolled along merrily and a few years after his divorce he met and married Audrey. Their union brought about a son called Aaron and shortly after that his other children returned to live with them both in Tasmania.

The underwater tales continued to flow thick and fast with Phil and it was not too long before he told me of his close encounters with sharks. He says learning how to control your fear and not let your heart rate start to race is the mark of a good diver, and he ought to know. Sharks make an audible noise when underwater, he tells me, when they make a turn and give their tail a flick. This creates a bubble that pops and creates a distinct noise. He recalls hearing that noise sometimes three times a day and knew that the louder the thump the bigger the shark. More often than not if you heard that sound it meant that you were being watched but he learned just to keep his head down and get on with his work. Of course, this is easier said than done, knowing you could be something's lunch at any minute.

Phil learned over the years to avoid diving at certain times of the year so as to avoid migrating schools of fish that of course, had bigger and less friendly ones following them. But even the smartest well-planned dives can't avoid the inevitable, and he has come as close as you can ever come to the apex predators of the oceans. On a particular day in the mid-seventies he was about seventy-five feet down peeling abalones off a sea wall in only about two feet of visibility, when all of a sudden he felt something big moving past. As he turned he just made out the intense black and white of a killer whale, which was probably no more than three feet away and definitely checking him out. As if that wasn't enough, the very next day, and in the same spot a giant grey thing 'slid past me where I was close enough that I could literally stare the beast straight in the eye.' It was certainly a White Pointer, he says, and at least four metres long. Suffice to say he returned to the surface pretty quickly and knocked off work for the rest of the day, feeling quite lucky to be alive.

His closest call came when he had an encounter with the biggest and ugliest hammerhead shark he'd ever seen.

'He must have been at least twelve feet long and seemed intent on making me his next meal. Luckily, I spied him far enough away to form some kind of defence and immediately rolled onto my back on the sea bed and put a large bag of the days catch between him and me. I watched him intently for a few minutes as he did figure of eights above me before eventually swimming away. At some point in that holding pattern the hammerhead was less than two feet above me and I could have easily punched it, but luckily, I think I chose to be a bit more passive in our brief relationship, which worked out well in the end. These experiences taught me to have a

*great respect for the ocean's bigger predators. You just never know
which way it's going to go when you encounter one and there is very
little you can do to alter your destiny.'*

Despite a full schedule of shark-wrestling Phil still
managed to find time to be a local hero and was involved
in one of the most dramatic rescues ever undertaken on the
little island of Tasmania. He recalls getting a call at 6am on
Mother's Day, 1985, to assist police trying to locate a canoeist
trying to cross Bass Strait. The man had left the day before but
had not thought to properly check the weather conditions. A
huge north-westerly storm came through in the night, and at
4.30am, in deep trouble, he put out a mayday call. Police rescue,
unfortunately, couldn't reach him because of the storm so they
asked Phil for help. Phil had helped them on previous occasions
so they knew he had a "big" boat moored at a local coastal
wharf. He was joined by a member of the local constabulary,
although they had no real idea as to where the lost kayaker was.
The sea got considerably rougher as they left the coast. Two
other boats joined the search and were trying to make their
way through huge waves of up to twelve metres, trying not
to capsize whilst still keeping an eye out for the missing man.
Phil had been diving that sea for many, many years and it still
remains one of the worst storms he's ever been caught up in.

Glancing over to another boat he saw it take a rogue wave
right on its port side and it rolled over. Not knowing how many
people were on board, or even having a plan ready, he changed
course and went to help the stricken vessel. As it transpired
there was a man clinging to each side of the vessel as it was
slowly sinking. During the difficult rescue attempt one guy had
swum off the boat to try and create room to pick him up. Phil's
deckhands and the policeman were at the rear of the boat trying
to encourage the man to grab the life ring. Phil turned his
attention to the remaining man as he was starting to drown. It
was a split-second decision he says and there was no option but
to jump in and drag him back to the capsized boat. So he yelled

to the boys to take the wheel, kicked his gumboots (galoshes) off and dived over the side into the freezing waters. Halfway to the drowning man a huge set of waves broke over everything. He dived under the first wave and saw that the man had been driven under and wasn't coming up. Just then two more waves, upwards of thirteen metres, broke around him, and more were following behind. Swimming to where he'd last seen the orange colour of the man's wet weather coat he dived down to find him numerous times but sadly he was unable to find the man. The capsized boat sank just seconds later and Phil's boat was drifting away downwind. It eventually went out of sight as he describes that last desperate moment…

'All I could do was tread water and, whenever a large wave came, I'd hold my arm up as the wave slid under me, hoping to be seen. I was at least twenty miles off the coast in huge seas, totally exhausted and close to drowning myself for the second time in my life, not to mention suffering the early stages of hypothermia. Finally, about twenty-five minutes later, my boat came along and luckily picked me up on its first attempt. They would have had to jump in and get me if they'd missed me as I was seconds from going under. All the guys on deck were in shock because they thought I'd drowned too, but had the presence of mind to just steam up into the wind and see if I was still there. I'll always be grateful that they did.'

The kayaker was located a few minutes after Phil was rescued, tied to his craft and floating around in the seas. He had clearly been dead for some time but no one wanted to risk a third death by trying to retrieve his body so the group headed back to safety. He still finds it hard to come to terms with it even now, over thirty years later – how one man's foolish actions cost him his life and the life of a man trying to save him.

There were a few repercussions after the rescue attempts. First, the channelling system didn't allow the search and rescue boats to communicate with the helicopters so the whole process was missing a vital link. This eventually led to the much improved rescue system that exists today. Phil was also nominated for two bravery awards – one being the *Star of Courage* which is the highest civilian award for bravery; and the other being the *Royal Humane Society* silver medal.

While some of Phil's stories certainly make great bedtime story material, I asked him if he ever kept anything from his children, given some of the serious situations he's been in. He believes that it is sometimes best to leave things at sea and not discuss moments that might cause them to worry. He recalls, in the early years when they were little, he would always say goodbye to them with an intensity and purpose that they would never understand because he always knew there was a chance he mightn't come back.

I ask him if he ever feels reflective about the way he parented given the perilous nature of his work. He laments that he thinks he did his best, given the person he was, and what he had experienced himself as a child. All he knew was that he didn't want the same upbringing he had for his own children. Perhaps, he says, he could have done things better but he's damn sure he did a better job than his dad and is happy if in turn his kids go on to say that they did a better job than him.

While some of Phil's stories don't always have the happiest of endings, he does have some amazing stories about his life and times in the fast lane as a younger man who was footloose and fancy-free. He was once headhunted by the United Kingdom's Fisheries' Ministry to do an exploratory dive in the Falkland Islands. During that posting he dived around almost two hundred islands and saw some of the most amazing shipwrecks he has ever seen. Although the operation discovered few commercial prospects, he did bear witness to sheep being used as land mine detectors.

Phil has, in later years, become something of a go-to man in terms of the raw surfing potential that Tasmania has to offer, and he has made a number of movies with some of Australia's most famous big wave legends including Tom Carroll and Ross

Clarke-Jones. As a film-maker you can read all the weather charts you like, and do all the research you want, but at the end of the day local knowledge rules, which is why Phil gets called upon as the unofficial gatekeeper of the west coast of Tasmania. It's been an experience that he has also been able to share with his two sons, Zeb and Aaron, as it's not every day your old man brings your childhood surfing heroes to your tiny home town.

Phil's home town of Marrawah has also staged two international competitions where some of the world's best surfers descended on the tiny town to compete. It was at one of these contests a few years back, when Phil was asked to accommodate one of Hawaii's living legends of surfing in 2000 World champion, Sunny Garcia and his wife, Colleen, who both came to stay at Phil and Audrey's farm. This, in turn, led to an invitation to Hawaii for the family, which happened to coincide with the most prestigious big wave contest in the world: the Eddie Aikau memorial contest to commemorate the life of Eddie Aikau, who lost his life trying the save the lives of others.

The event kicks off with a paddle out at Waimea Bay where all the invited contestants from around the world take to the water and link hands in a giant circle to honour Eddie Aikau. As far as my research could turn up, the paddle out is a competitors-only affair, which is strictly policed, but somehow Phil became the first-ever non-competitor to be invited to take part in the opening ceremony, which is kind of along the same lines as getting invited to a NASA "who's been to the Moon party", without ever having set foot in a rocket.

When it comes to guys like Phil who have spent time in worlds that few people get to see, I like to ask, just out of interest, if there is anything that scares them about the world. While he's clearly fairly fearless, he alludes to the fact that he is, in fact, quite worried about the environmental impact that humans are having on the world. He's seen the changes underwater with his own eyes over a fifty-year period.

'Yes, I've seen some pretty big changes in nature over my many years diving. Tasmania is very close to the damaged part of the ozone layer that you hear so much about and I can tell you, without a shadow of a doubt, that the increased UV spectrum has put pressure on and depleted huge beds of Macrocystis (floating kelp) and virtually wiped it out in our part of the world. Fertiliser run-off has also had a really profound affect and produced huge areas of green weeds and algae. Once fertilisers reach the ocean the many nutrients they do contain, including high levels of nitrogen, are released into the water. Normally, marine ecosystems do contain some of these nutrients that these fertilisers are made up of as they help marine plants, including algae, to grow. However, when such strong levels of the nutrients are released, some algae species explode in growth and clog up the food chain.'

It does, in some ways, paint a bleak future. But it's important for Phil to lead by example and live an eco-friendly life. The farm he lives on with his wife is almost totally run off solar and wind power and the family is very passionate about their lifestyle. He thinks about the coming generations and what kind of world they will inherit.

He admits that he has been lucky in life but hopefully given back as much as he's taken. While he doesn't dive with sharks any more he still rides the big waves off the west coast of Tasmania, and the occasional "medium" sized ones whenever he visits his friends in Hawaii.

His story in a way reminds you in a way about the old cliché about living life to the full and not letting anything get in the way of your dreams. He's been to the pearly gates before and has no intention of going back there anytime soon. One suspects as well that a new adventure could happen at any minute but hopefully he'll wait until the sea is a little calmer before throwing himself off the side of the boat again.

"Giving a master class"

XIV
THE HIGH-WIRE WALKER

©Tom de Peyret

Heights are a strange phenomenon when it comes to fear. It's unclear what really occurs in a person's life that determines whether they will be scared of heights, as humans aren't born with that fear inbuilt. Perhaps for those who fear heights, more of the apprehension is down to fear of the consequences rather than the height itself. Let's say you stand in your driveway and lay a long thick sturdy plank of wood in front of you. The plank is a foot wide and only eight feet long so you'd have no trouble walking from one end to the other, would you? Take that same plank and raise it ten feet above the ground between two ladders, and we have a completely different scenario. What everyone found really easy to do on the ground suddenly becomes unachievable for many, once the proverbial bar is raised.

So what makes the difference? Is it the fear of the height or the fear of falling from the height, or perhaps a little of both? If you were to think of heights and activities that involved heights, then something along the lines of a high-wire act or tightrope walker is going to be right up there. It's more than likely that you have seen one at a circus or a festival somewhere in your youth. Circuses really aren't what they used to be though. Certainly, in the last few years, the vast majority of travelling shows featuring animals have all but vanished. This maybe a function of animal rights or just a natural shift in what the paying public want to see. What has replaced the traditional Big Top show is a resurgence in the art of acrobatics and other highly skilled, daring trades of circus entertainment such as high-wire walking. That, coupled with the popularity of extreme sports in general, has seen the whole industry of "spectacle" becoming as mainstream as any other physical pursuit.

Jade Kindar-Martin has been involved in entertainment since he was a young boy and is now somewhat of a legend in the industry. When it comes to people like Jade, and the unique jobs they do, it's equally amazing to discover the path they took to become what they are, as much as the career itself. Did he ever think about running away with the circus, for example? It turns out that wasn't a million miles away from the truth.

Most young boys like to climb trees, and the young Jade was certainly no different. He recalls when he was six years old climbing up the side of his house and perching on the chimney to look around and take it all in. He says there was something a bit mystical about being up that high and being able to see life from such a unique angle. Of course, at some point his mother was going to come looking for him, wondering where he had got to. He remembers hearing his mother calling for him and coming outside to find him. She walked out the front door and looked up, whereby the young boy waved to her and she waved back to him. She asked him quite calmly what he was doing up there and he replied that he was just looking around. Jade says she didn't tell him to come back down, only to be careful.

His mother clearly had quite a few more such experiences to the extent that eight years later she asked him if he wanted to audition for a youth circus camp called *Circus Smirkus*. It was started by a clown who had worked in European circuses. Jade auditioned for a spot and was accepted and the rest, they say, is history. Jade says the circus was set up extraordinarily well and had a large tent which served as their practice area, their meeting place, and where they used to perform their shows. It was quite a fast learning curve as they only had three weeks to rehearse before they took the show on the road. That first show toured for a month and the children did two shows a day, six days a week. By the end of it Jade had done almost seventy shows and he looks back on it now with great nostalgia as the most amazing experience of his young life.

He learned not only about how a circus is run, but also about responsibility. He also learned how to sew costumes, to keep his space and wire clean, and make sure his props were all in order. That regimented style and structure, he says, gave him a solid grounding and led to the success he has had in his later years. *Circus Smirkus*, he tells me, is still running to this day some thirty years after the first original show and he's delighted to know that there are still children out there getting to experience the same things he did as a child.

As far as jobs go in life, he's created a fairly amazing one for himself. It's one thing to enjoy something that is a little on the dangerous and quirky side, but it's another to have the mindset and dedication to actually turn it into one that pays the bills.

Jade was lucky enough to be schooled by Rudy Oman-kowsky Jr., commonly recognised as the grand master of the high-wire. Rudy comes from a very long line of high-wire walkers, eight generations in fact, if you can believe that. As Rudy has no children of his own, he and Jade have a slight father/son relationship. It's also Rudy's wish that Jade and his other apprentices pass down the tradition on his behalf.

The more you read into the education Jade has had on the wire, the more it seems like a kind of Peter Pan story. There was, as mentioned, the circus from a young age, and then after graduating from high school he had a stint at the *École National de Cirque* in Canada before going on to study at the *Centre National des Arts du Cirque* in France.

The young Jade does not seem to have been too bothered with school in the traditional sense of the word. You get the feeling that his entrance and exit to high school was simply an interlude in the career that he already had planned. Most people don't know what they want to do before high school, and maybe even fewer do once they've left, so it's quite impressive to show such focus at such a young age.

To your average person, the idea of walking on a wire is probably not the most enticing activity, as they can quite easily imagine just how dangerous it is and what could go wrong. I would have thought the "falling off" part would be the anxiety-inducing part of the whole thing. Even if you manage to hang on by your hands how exactly do you get back up? Do you just hang there and wait till the strength goes, and fall to your thudding demise? A recurring theme throughout these pages is that these guys are simply unafraid, and for the most part believe themselves to be in control of the situation, and Jade, as the *High-wire Walker Extraordinaire*, is no different.

Jade's first real move into the limelight actually came as a duo when he joined forces with Didier Pasquette, another famous high-wire aficionado. Didier was also trained by Jade's mentor, Rudy, so they had a very close connection. Both of them have also been lucky enough to spend time with Philippe Petit, another grand master of the high wire. His name may not mean much to you but his feats might ring a bell. He was the man who did an unauthorised walk between the Twin Towers in New York City back in 1974. He didn't just do it once and let it go though, as he stuck around to entertain the crowds below for some forty-five minutes and crossed back and forth some eight times before the show was called to a close. If you've a mortal fear of heights like me then you'll be shuddering at the thought of a man balancing on a wire some four hundred metres above the ground by what have now become the most iconic, destroyed buildings in history. Philippe was taken to task by the law over his "reckless" actions, but thankfully all charges were dropped in return for him performing for a children's event in Central Park. He's still alive and kicking today and lives in the same city where he made his name all those years ago.

Returning to Jade, he clearly took a leaf out of the book of his high-wire "ancestors". Together with Didier they formed a formidable partnership that spanned six years through their early twenties into their thirties. Their most daring walk together was actually over the River Thames in London in 1997, in which they traversed the 1,200ft between the Oxo Tower on the South Bank and the HMS Wellington, which was moored on the Victoria Embankment. Using poles to balance, they set out from opposite sides of the river, some one hundred and fifty feet in the air, and with safety harnesses. From that height, falling and hitting the water could easily have killed them. Even had they survived the fall, the Thames is not a forgiving river.

The unique aspect of their walk, which gained them a world record, was that no one had ever carried out such a walk with both walkers on the same wire travelling in opposite directions towards each other. The question, of course, is what happens when you meet in the middle? It's not like there is a lay-by as in the side of the road. Our dynamic duo solved that with a minimal amount of fuss: Didier sat down carefully on the wire and Jade stepped carefully over him and went on his way. It was quite a sight to behold and you could see why they went on to have such success together… Synchronicity at its finest. Though their partnership ended in 1998, they remain close.

The continual lure of the circus loomed too great, and in 1999 Jade joined the *Cirque du Soleil* in Florida. That franchise is by far the most well known in the world and they only recruit the best, so Jade's star was certainly rising. While he turned the heads of the crowd it appeared there was someone a bit more special, part of his troupe, that caught his eye, a young lady called Karine. She was an amazing acrobat and gymnast and you couldn't have asked for a more perfect partnership.

It's one thing to find a partner who shares similar interests but to fall in love with someone who does a similar, relatively obscure job as you, must be quite a coup. It probably won't sound too unbelievable to find out that the pair actually exchanged vows on the high-wire itself, which certainly isn't something that happens every day. Karine had never walked the high wire before she met Jade, and hasn't walked it since the wedding, but it was kind of what you might call *learning to dance,* as many couples do for their wedding, but with just a slight touch more of edginess.

The marriage itself brought three children within a decade – Raphael, Gabriel and Jophielle who are twelve, eight and four respectively. While you may have thought that this could have slowed the career of Mrs Kindar-Martin, I'm afraid to say that it only seemed to give it more propulsion. She is now a very successful Hollywood stuntwoman and the list of people she's played on screen is quite impressive. She's been Dakota Fanning in Steven Spielberg's *War of the Worlds*, Emma Roberts in *Nancy Drew* and even played an elf in the very successful *Polar Express.* Talk about meeting your match!

I'm intrigued at what kind of conversation occurs around the dinner table of this family *extraordinaire*… How do you discuss life prospects with your children when both husband and wife effectively walk out the front door into perpetual danger?

Jade says he and Karine discuss much more than the dangers of either of their chosen careers. They find risk every day in the world around them, but he feels safest when on his wire. It may sound cheesy, but Jade definitely thinks that navigating this world and keeping his children safe is a lot riskier than walking on a steel cable hundreds of feet in the air, or Karine being flung through the air like a rag doll for that matter. Jade and Karine understand that their children have never known anything different so it's perfectly normal to them. Their kids have effectively grown up within a *circus of a circus*, which is probably the best way to describe it to an outsider. What's more, all their friends are children of their parents' friends who are in the industry so they think it's pretty normal as well.

'Karine and I have, of course, spoken about the possibility of death,' he tells me, 'but we made an agreement some time ago that we would only use our energies to worry about ourselves and not the other, as there is no way we can help to keep each other safe by using worry as a tool. My children and I have talked about death. I simply try to instil in them a sense or belief that death is not an ending, but a continuation of matter and energy in the universal sense. I guess I believe life is just a cycle and it's just one more step on the path to where we, as a universal consciousness, are going.'

He has vaguely mentioned that he might like his ashes scattered from a mountainside, but is only planning that to be a ceremony his grown-up children attend and not something for the foreseeable future.

Jade's current main focus is what he calls the *FireWire*, which is pretty much exactly what you think it is. Basically, the wire is on fire while he walks on it, as if it wasn't hard enough as it is. It's become his trademark in a sense, and he builds his whole persona around it as a spectacle. He performs this stunt all around the world and explains the challenge of getting himself halfway around the globe with all his equipment in tow. The rigging involved in setting up a high-wire isn't overly complex but it must be done absolutely perfectly every time to ensure the tension is correct. The gas that fuels the flame can also be challenging as gases vary greatly from country to country meaning that what he's walking on in one place might be quite a lot hotter in another. Accordingly, he has to have special boots made that will protect his feet but still give him enough feel on the wire to find his way.

A few years back Jade also belonged to a high-wire act called *The Flying Wallendas*. It was originally started by a family of that name that continues this tradition today. They do however, accept outsiders with special talents, and this is where Jade used to be a hired gun, so to speak. His work with them involved performing what is called the *Seven Man Pyramid*. Effectively, that involved four people standing balancing on the wire with two separate poles balanced on each pair's shoulders. On top of those planks stand another two people with another pole on their shoulders and a final person on top of that. So basically it's a walking pyramid. It certainly looks extraordinarily dangerous and difficult, doubly so when you realise that they don't use a safety net. Apparently this goes against the traditions of the Wallendas and they like to keep it very, very real. You would think if you were a high-wire walker that you might try to get a safer second job, like that of a shelf stocker, but not Jade. He simply went out and found a fill-in job for a while that was even more dangerous than the one he already had.

'I'm aware that what Karine and I do for a living is seen as somewhat exotic by the general public, but I just look at myself as an entertainer and an artist. The only time I ever notice the contrast of what I do for a living, and let's say normal life, is immediately after I arrive back home after doing a big show. When I get back from a job or a trip I feel like I have to run around and do things at a million miles an hour. It takes me a while to be able

to just relax and come down off the high of a performance. I might be mowing the lawn or picking up the dog poop in the backyard and I think to myself… "Yesterday I was performing in front of a prince or a sultan or one million people and today I'm mowing the lawn and doing regular stuff". Of course that strangeness always passes, but if anything, I've always found it amusing when those two worlds collide.'

Jade rebukes me on a few occasions for calling what he does dangerous. He thinks it's a misconception about his profession. In fact he considers that he and his fellow walkers are so well trained and proficient at what they do that the majority of the risk is all but removed. I had always wondered to myself what would happen to a high-wire walker should they put a foot wrong and find themselves in a precarious position on the wire, or worse still, dangling by their hands. I get the feeling when I ask this question that he is somewhat amused. Bar a low flying bird or lightning hitting him mid-walk, he says it's fairly unlikely he will ever find himself in a position where he is dangling by his hands having lost his balancing pole. He does say that, of course, there is a chance that he could put a foot wrong but that would more than likely mean he'd end up in a crumpled position on the wire while still clutching his pole.

I guess what you have to remember is that these guys have insane balancing abilities even when faced with unplanned events and are able to correct themselves fairly easily. I do press him, though, on what would happen in the event that he did end up dangling. He says that in that unlikely event he would swing himself up and hook one leg over the wire and try and make his way to the nearest *cavalletti* – which are the wires that hold the main wire steady from the side. If he ever got into that position he would simply slide down the nearest side wire and to safety.

The talk of danger stirs his memory though, and he tells me a tale of when he was riding a special Giraffe unicycle (in layman's terms this is a really tall unicycle) on the wire and it all went a bit wrong. He tells the story of getting his pant leg caught in the chain of the unicycle. Normally he would ride along the wire on the unicycle and jump down onto to the wire in the middle, and the unicycle would fall into a small hand-held net below. This particular time, before he came to his normal spot he faced a problem because if he jumped off with his pants caught in the chain the weight of the unicycle would pull him down off the wire. So he had to carefully pedal backwards, and uphill (something that that particular bike is not designed for) to unhook the errant pant leg. Didier was not on the wire at the time. He was on the platform and he could only watch on helplessly. Thankfully he got himself out of trouble but if he hadn't, he can't be sure how serious the consequences might have been.

Jade considers that it was growing up without a consistent father figure in his life that has made him the person he is, although he's not sure if that's more resilient or self-reliant. His own children have certainly benefited from his involvement in their lives, although not always, as he once almost drowned them all. It is, he says, his most epic fail as a father. It was actually fairly clear-cut and may have, unfortunately, instilled the fear of open water and sail boating in his two sons.

The family were on vacation on the Isle of Wight, on the south coast of the United Kingdom. They had rented a lovely stone cottage which had a backyard and a little open gateway which gave them direct access to the beach, and they also had two sailboats. He'd been sailing since he was young and had lived around lakes all his life. He took the boat out for a sail with his wife and children. When they were too far to swim back, Karine suddenly noticed water was starting to pool heavily in the bottom of the boat. Jade quickly realised that the boat was sinking, and quite quickly. To cut a long story short they ended up being saved by a man and his son in a motor boat who, out of sheer luck happened to be passing by, and who towed them back to the shore.

Had it been closer to dark, or had no one been around, he only shudders at what might have happened. Now back on the shore and wondering what the hell happened Jade checked the boat and saw that the bung (the drain plug in the hull of the boat) was out, let out by himself no less! Needless to say he's never quite lived that one down, and although he recalls that Karine didn't say too much at the time, he does remember vividly the expression on her face when they realised the whole affair had been his doing. Fortunately, the lucky escape wasn't lost on him, and he has used the memory of it to be more vigilant ever since.

Jade has an interesting way of compartmentalising fear.

'When I'm on the wire, I am Jade the High-wire Walker, and for the duration of the show I cease in a sense to be I, Jade the father, the husband, the son, and the friend. Fear is, and must be, categorized. It cannot be allowed to get out of control. That is where things go astray. I look at wire walking from an artist's perspective, from a rigger's perspective, from a professional's perspective. Sometimes I will try to see it through the spectators' eyes. But the fear that paralyses and inhibits is born out of the unknown and once we have identified the risks there is only the show that is left. It is a hard concept to explain but it remains the sole reason I've been able to do what I do for so long. Having the ability to reprogram your mind to perform tasks that your everyday persona might question is a common and valuable tool in the bag of the high-wire walker.'

However, he doesn't shield his children from his own escapades. They often let the older children walk on the big wire, with a safety harness of course. He doesn't necessarily want them to follow in his footsteps but it would be nice, he thinks, if one of them did. He hopes to pass the tradition down to the next generation of his family and is very excited about the possibility of that happening. But for the moment Jade is still very much a performer.

In 2015 Jade appeared in *The Walk*, a big budget film directed by Robert Zemeckis of *Back to the Future* fame. The events of the film were based on the aforementioned Twin Towers walk. It was a role tailor-made for Jade as he just happens to be the exact same height and build as the film's star, Joseph Gordon-Levitt. His casting was somewhat of a fluke though, as somebody who was working on the early stage production of the film remembered that Karine, who was around movie sets all the time, had a husband who was a high-wire walker.

The movie really is worth a watch and the backstory about the preparations they did to make it happen are truly amazing. Perhaps one of the most interesting logistics depicted in the film is how they got the wire from building to building but I don't want to spoil the plot. Jade says Karine was really the one who knew how show business worked and how to conduct oneself on set while he was somewhat of a newbie to that world, walking around bumping into things and not understanding the process. At one point he asked the assistant director for a cup of coffee, as well as asking the caterer what he thought of the camera angle. He described himself as literally one of those country bumpkins new to a city with eyes as wide as saucers.

Not long after the movie started filming though, his third child (his first daughter) was born. Luckily he had negotiated with the producers that he was to be flown back to France for forty-eight hours so that he could assist with the birth of his child. He says he actually left thirty-six hours after arriving in France and was back on set, having barely drawn breath – from one high to another and then back again.

He'll never forget how surreal it was to see himself up on the silver screen during the premiere. He only hopes that he brought honour to his profession and made the people who took the time to teach him along the way proud. Although Jade didn't actually do a walk between the towers but to people who ask if he would have done it if given the chance, he responds that it would have been an honour to attempt the most famous high-wire walk of all.

For now, though, life is good for Jade, and his young family continue to thrive. He has all that he ever wanted and a successful international career to go with it. The family divides their time between the USA and France and he is always planning his next big stunt.

"Fire in the night sky"

XV
THE PARATROOPER

'Paratroopers are unique in that they are expected to fight while surrounded by the enemy, with the smallest of arms against huge odds…and win.' This probably doesn't sound like the best way to advertise this unique military career. However in a nutshell it sums up perfectly what is involved and paints a very clear picture of exactly the kind of people that are the distinct breed the military calls Paratroopers.

Paratroopers are essentially Airborne Military Units, usually consisting of light infantry and a variety of support arms such as helicopters, light artillery, air defence and armour. They are trained to be moved by aircraft and "dropped" into battle wherever needed. Paratroopers bring a unique dimension to battles as they can be placed behind enemy lines quite easily and have the capability to deploy almost anywhere with little warning. It is this surprise factor that has struck fear into the enemy since 1918. As a German officer wrote in World War II –

"American parachutists…devils in baggy pants…are less than a hundred meters from my outpost line. I can't sleep at night; they pop up from nowhere and we never know when or how they will strike next. Seems like the black-hearted devils are everywhere…"

This distinct deployment capability allows military commanders to dispatch either small Special Operations Teams or much larger groups if required in various aircraft over the years. It was possible to fit up to 152 paratroopers in one plane for a single deployment. In effect the equivalent of a small army descending from the skies behind enemy lines.

Strategically, Airborne Operations gives a commander the capability of putting a fighting force on the ground quickly to secure key areas of the battlefield such as bridges, road junctions and blocking positions along the enemy's major avenues. It is seen as a way to cut the blood lines of the enemy by disabling his means of transport and confusing its chain of command. To say it's a dangerous profession would be a bit of an understatement. For a start they need to be dropped in or near an actual battle. Doing this via parachute, and often at night, only adds another layer of danger. Even with the best intelligence available of the enemy, its position and numbers are not always accurate, so they are often descending into the unknown.

Due to jumping factors they are restricted to carrying only small amounts of munitions or weaponry. Essentially they are trained to fight the enemy with minimal resources. It's worth mentioning that despite the existence of paratrooper regiments, they are not deployed on a regular basis as the situations that demand their presence occur rarely.

Colonel Gordon Sumner was a highly decorated paratrooper and aviator in the US Army. He served in various roles in many different countries over a twenty-seven-year period, including a lengthy stint in the British Army where he also became highly decorated. On the ground he has fought in handgun-drawn 'man-on-man' firefights where he was once almost fatally wounded. He has some two hundred and fifty field jumps under his belt. He served as the Commanding Officer for two units within his paratrooper division where he was both revered and respected by his peers. Looking at his medals of valour and awards, one can't quite believe that there are that many military awards or decorations in existence. There are a swathe of US and British Army awards: the Secretary of Defense Medal for Exceptional Public Service; the Commandant of the Coast Guard Distinguished Civilian Service Medal; People of Distinction commendations, as well as humanitarian accolades. My eyes scan for the Purple Heart Medal, and sure enough it's there as well. Gordon has done some pretty serious service throughout his career. Given the sheer number of times he saw action and the danger involved each time, he was either a very lucky solider or a seriously talented and efficient one. Perhaps it was a bit of both.

Paratroopers can feel like sitting ducks between jumping from a plane and landing on enemy territory. They are often quite easy to spot as they fall to the ground and truly easy targets when within range of standard hand-held munitions. Hollywood films portray them as drawing guns and shooting back at the enemy below, but this is a somewhat unrealistic portrayal as the parachutes are smaller than standard parachutes and a lot harder to control, so both hands are required to properly guide yourself down. Trying to shoot at someone on the ground from the air would be a little like swinging around on a clothes line one-handed and trying to hit a tin can a hundred yards away. James Bond could certainly do it but being a paratrooper isn't a job of make-believe.

During WWII, those paratroopers that jumped with weapons in hand often lost their weapons as they were yanked away from them as they exited the aircraft. The jump isn't always easy and one needs to be in excellent physical condition to be able to steer the chute for landing through all types of weather. That's assuming you exit the plane without any problems.

Gordon related how one time he jumped too far out from the door of a C-141 Starlifter and was slammed by the jet blast of the plane into the side and tail section of the aircraft more than once. The blow knocked him out for a few seconds but fortunately he was not badly injured, regained consciousness and was able to land safely. Despite a few knocks, Gordon enjoyed his moments in the air. He was known to take an old Kodak Instamatic camera with him to take photos as his soldiers exited the plane. Perhaps a precurser to the modern day "selfie", although perhaps slightly more dangerous than usual.

Although military service in his family goes back a few generations, Gordon was the first in his family to serve as a paratrooper.

'We have a long lineage of military history dating back to the American Revolution. I have had a direct descendant in uniform in every major conflict and some minor conflicts since the Revolutionary War! And, we have had a direct descendant in uniform continually since 1941, including my daughter. The strength, encouragement, and prayers from my family are paramount to the success I've experienced during my life.'

It's difficult not to want to find out about Gordon's time served with the British Army Air Corps as it's such a unique thing to have done as an American citizen, especially during the period when a war of independence was waging in Northern Ireland. It was certainly an opportunity for him and his family to experience a different way of life. The world today is awash with news of terrorist attacks but back when Gordon arrived to serve for another country, he had neither experienced terrorist attacks on home soil nor had his family ever been targetted. As he describes…

'The difference serving with the British Army was that the IRA was attacking both the military and family members. It was truly my first experience with terrorists. Those individuals who, to me, had no respect for life and were only killing to make their political points known; coupled with losing soldiers to these killers, I had no reservations that when given an opportunity, I would do likewise to them.'

One of the means that the IRA employed to try and kill those on base was to place bombs under the cars of serving officers. Every morning within the confines of the base they'd have to check the cars for bombs, strange wires, or anything out of the ordinary.

'It sounds like something from a Hollywood movie but these were the threats we faced every single day. There were many lucky escapes through our diligence that was encapsulated in our training.'

It's worth mentioning that at this time that the people in Gordon's position were slightly lucky in that the Internet was not not yet a source of information: while it took the IRA some 30 years to make the jump from rudimentary explosives to complex ones, it took modern day groups like ISIS a mere two years.

On one occasion, the IRA blew up the Officers' Mess at a base located not too far from the airfield where Gordon was stationed. It took place during a dinner to which Gordon had been invited but had been unable to attend. Gordon looks back now certainly at his career and knows he was luckier than some. This fact has never been lost on him. The statistics of war and its casualties sometimes hide the human side to the loss of life. Facts and figures can sometimes cloak the fact that for every person that dies there is a swathe of people close to that person who are forever changed.

'What many people don't realise is that as a fighting unit you're not simply fighting for a country, not fighting for a flag or even for patriotism. You're fighting simply for the guys beside you. Those who have chosen to serve alongside you. It is truly a band of brothers and sisters.'

Over the course of the interview, Gordon often speaks about the responsibility of leadership and the difficulties of leading men into battle. There is always the distinct and very real possibility that as they cascade like dominoes out of the plane's hull, not all will return. He is very proud to be able to say, and I expect somewhat relived, that he never lost a single man in any facet of training or battle. That's not to say that there haven't been some serious injuries to the men under his care. With almost an audible wince in his voice he describes a soldier whose parachute partially failed and who plummeted to the ground at a fair speed. Luckily on that occasion, and in almost a freaky fashion, he landed in a shallow pond with a soft mud bottom and managed to crawl away with "only" a pair of broken ankles. With a deep sigh Gordon says it was always a satisfying feeling to see troops return safely home to their families. They all knew the risks and he's enterally grateful for not having to directly suffer any loss of life while he was a squadron leader.

Men like Gordon were born in a different era and you can't help but think that a portion of the stiff upper lip that the British are famous for rubbed off on him during his service in the UK. I asked Gordon if he ever felt guilty about raising his daughter, Andrea (Ande), in the midst of conflict and uprooting her from various schools when he was deployed to different parts of the world. He doesn't need to explain that they are a very close father and daughter unit. She believes she learned much from her time on the move and that it was a very positive influence on her life. She learned about different people, traditions, cultures, foods, languages and most of all, respect for those men and women who put their lives on the line to fight for their country. In true testament to the positive influence her father had on her, Ande also chose to serve in the military as well, not as a paratrooper, but as a physician assistant in the US Air Force.

I asked him if he ever had a discussion with his significant other before they decided to have children. He explained that even before Ande was born both he and his wife, Vicki, understood the expectations of the job and the risks involved, including wild cards such as no-notice deployments, potential combat tours and training or in-the-field accidents. There was also the real possibility of him not seeing his child for months at a time, but it was something they both decided was just part and parcel of what he did and that they would work around it as best they could.

Being the best dad you can through any circumstance is always a challenge, but for military dads it's just that little bit harder. Many of the fellow daredevils in this book get to choose their battles and where they are fought, but for dads like Gordon the battles are chosen for them and they have to adapt to be the fathers they want to be in sometimes very challenging situations.

While stationed in West Germany with the 3rd Armoured Division he recalls vividly a conversation he had with his Brigade Commander discussing the other mans upcoming twin sons' birthdays. It was a bit of a fleeting conversation between two guys just shooting the breeze. The Commander mentioned that he didn't really remember much of both boys growing up as he wasn't there for a lot of it, for one reason or another. Gordon thought at the time that he didn't ever want to be in that position or ever be that kind of dad. Ande and he would not be strangers during her childhood years, and that was a decision he made pretty much in that moment, at a time when she was just a three year old whom he was still just getting to know.

So the promise was made to her, and to himself, pretty much then and there that when not deployed, he would ensure that they had their own special time each week, their "Daddy/ Daughter" night.

'My wife was doing such a fantastic job raising her through the ups and downs of being a military wife that she was happy to let us have our special time together and put her well-travelled feet up for a while. This was also an indirect benefit of doing what I did, and my commitment to being as hands-on a dad as I could be, It only made my own relationship with my wife all the better.'

Gordon is clearly not your typical military man, although he is very much tough as nails. His sense of humour probably kept him sane through almost three decades of service. With a name name like his (Sting's name is Gordon Sumner) he certainly needed a sense of humour. He jokingly says that over the years there has always been a degree of disappointment when he turns up to a restaurant or other function, especially in the UK. When you share the same unique name as a well-known rock n' roll superstar, it's inevitable that the gossip mill will explode prior to your arrival. It's just something he has gotten used to and he takes it in his stride. Although he might never have been in a famous band he certainly had a glittering career of his own.

Time has taken its toll on Gordon's body. The impacts of landing hundreds and hundreds of times onto hard ground, whilst weighed down by gear, can wreak havoc on the human skeleton. It's almost unheard of for a paratrooper not to have experienced some kind of back issues. Gordon candidly remarks that he has in fact had two vertebrae replaced as a result of constant pain. Surprisingly though, he's been told by various people within the medical community that the pain has as much to do with what he wears during operations as it does with the jumping. Wearing heavy aviation helmets as well as night vision goggles for thousands of helicopter flight hours in the air puts immense strain on the spine and that takes its toll.

No matter how respectful I want to be in questioning Gordon, it's impossible not to want to ask about Post Traumatic Stress Disorder (PTSD) and whether he has been affected by it. Although he admits he doesn't truly know or believe if he has suffered from it, he thinks it's certainly possible. He says that depending on whom you talk with, some medical folks believe that just about anyone who has been in combat has some degree of PTSD. It is said that the incidence of PTSD rises sharply for anyone with a Purple Heart and that those medal recipients could suffer some degree of PTSD.

He says he finds comfort and solace being with his fellow Purple Heart veterans and having the ability to talk with them when he needs to just talk, or just simply listen. Having all been wounded in combat, they all know that while they might have left the battlefield, the battle may not have left them.

At times throughout the process of Gordon becoming part of this book there were many moments when it was difficult to coax information from him. True heroes, you see, have a tendency to gloss over their heroism. Gordon knows that for every high moment you might have had as a soldier there is the low moment for another soldier who wasn›t so lucky. You can›t, however, hand a writer a sheet of paper that lists a Purple Heart Medal on it and expect to explain it away in two sentences... which he tried to do. We both agreed that I should be allowed to respectfully tell the story for him to give it the attention it deserves, and the following excerpt is my interpretation of what happened on the night he earned the ultimate medal the US military can bestow on a courageous soldier who is killed or wounded in battle.

While stationed on the island Grenada, during Operation Fury in 1983, Gordon's base came under attack from the People's Revolutionary Army. Given the nature of where they were stationed they had established a perimeter defence of the base and had placed their main guns along the most likely avenues of approach into and out of that area. It was a fairly volatile time in that part of the world and they expected to be attacked at any time, night or day. On that particular night after carrying out the usual checks on base, Gordon had gone to bed when the perimeter was attacked. When he heard the first sounds of gunfire, he and his First Sergeant jumped up from their bunks and headed to the area they considered to be that of the main action. This is probably the part that's a bit hard to grasp from someone who has never been a part of war, because when you are stationed in the middle of it you're always on edge and battle-ready, and there is no running for cover. As he ran towards the sound of gunfire with pistol drawn he was hit by a bullet in his left leg. He didn't realise what had happened and thought he had just stumbled and fallen. The firefight continued for a little while but he couldn't recall how long he was down – now wounded – and did his best to continue commanding the unit as it fended off the enemy shot after shot.

After it all ended they had killed a few men from the People's Revolutionary Army and also captured a couple of Cuban military advisors. Gordon recounts that it was probably adrenaline – a chemical that the body dishes out in order to help you carry on in moments of absolute peak endurance – that got him through that battle. He never even knew he had been shot and it was only when his First Sergeant noticed that he was bleeding that he even realised that he was wounded on and just above his knee. It's on this point that he laments that he never really understood why the Purple Heart Medal was bestowed on him as he was only doing what he had to do, to protect the base and the men whom he served with. What's more it wasn't a serious wound either.

We ended the discussion on the topic with the mention of degrees. A gust of wind or a millisecond later in movement might have resulted in that gunshot just tapering a little higher up the leg than would have been ideal, and may have excluded

Colonel Sumner from being eligible for a role in this book for pretty obvious reasons.

I had to do the math myself, but in 1983 our heroic paratrooper was still only a recently married man who was yet to receive the call of fatherhood. Whichever way you look at it, either he was very lucky to have been a father or his daughter was very lucky to have been a part of the world.

Such are the perils of life as a military dad that it's very satisfying to find a man who is so humble in his heroics, so very capable as a soldier and so dedicated a family man. As the years since his service has passed and that little girl has grown into a woman he's never lost touch with his roots and men with whom he shared service. He travels regularly on the military circuit and lends support where he can. It's something that's very important to him and solidifies the bond between himself and his fellow veterans. Perhaps it's only a bond that people who have been into battle can share with each other. Either way that bond is there for life for men like Gordon as they put their lives on the line.

"Diving into the war zone"

If you have enjoyed this book, the author would love it if you could leave a review on Amazon, or on the channel through which you purchased this copy.